Blessed Are the Peacemakers

FOR THEY WILL BE CALLED CHILDREN OF GOD."

Devotional Messages
July-December 2008

Blessed Are the Peacemakers
Copyright © (2010) by Paula J Behrens
All rights reserved

Reverend Paula J Behrens is a full membership Elder in the
Texas Annual Conference of the United Methodist Church,
Ordained in 2007. She graduated from *Houston Baptist
University* with a *Bachelor of Arts* degree in Christianity and
English and acquired her *Master of Divinity* from *Perkins School
of Theology*, Southern Methodist University.

Reverend Behrens has served as pastor in six United Methodist congregations. She is currently appointed as the Senior Pastor of Chappell Hill United Methodist Church in Chappell Hill, Texas. She has three grown children and three grandchildren. Her desire is to use her gifts and graces in such a way as to bring as much glory to God's kingdom as possible in this lifetime.

Her desire is to use her gifts and graces in such a way as to bring as much glory to God's kingdom as possible in this lifetime.

This collection of messages is lovingly
dedicated to my children:
Sharleen Manning
Bruce Behrens, Jr.
Nicholas Behrens

My siblings:
Cathy Behrens
Bobby Acree
Sylvia Thomas

And the members of:
Chappell Hill United Methodist Church
5195 Church Street/ PO Box 285
Chappell Hill, TX 77426
(979) 836-7795
www.chappellhillumc.org

Blessed Are the Peacemakers

Table of Contents

SCRIPTURE INDEX

OLD TESTAMENT

Genesis 45:1-15
Isaiah 40:1-11
Revelation 5:1-14

NEW TESTAMENT

Matthew 8:1-17
Matthew 11:25-30
Matthew 13:1-9, 18-23
Matthew 13:31-32; 44-52
Matthew 14:22-33
Matthew 14:13-21
Matthew 16:21-25
Matthew 16:21-28
Matthew 18:15-20
Matthew 20:1-16
Matthew 21:23-32
Matthew 22:1-14
Matthew 23:1-12
Matthew 25:1-13
Mark 5:21-43
Mark 10:17-25
Luke 1:26-38
Luke 13:1-9
John 1:6-14
Acts 9:32-42
Romans 12:1-8
2 Corinthians 9:6-15

Preface

There once was a little girl who attended church only because her parents dropped her and her siblings off for Sunday school and worship every week. Now, this was a good thing, because at least she did have a chance to hear about the love of God. But it was not the best thing, because her parents never joined them for worship and that influenced how she thought about God.

What happened is this little girl grew up thinking that church was only for children. And she reasoned, just as soon as she was grown, well, she wouldn't have to go to church any more. And that's exactly what happened, once she was grown, she did as her parents had done, dropping her own three children off for Sunday school and church, and seldom attending herself. It was her understanding that she was an adult and adults didn't need anyone's help (not even God's). She could and would take care of herself.

She had been taught that if she just worked hard enough, she would be able to get all the things she needed, all the things that would bring happiness and contentment into her life. It might take a while, she thought, but she could do it. And so she worked very hard at acquiring all the things she needed and all the things she wanted, and by the age of forty she had most all of them: a nice house, a faithful husband and three beautiful children.

But guess what, she wasn't happy, she wasn't content. At her dismay, she sensed that there was something missing. She didn't quite know what it was, but she knew something was missing. It seemed that there was this strange emptiness in her life. It was like she had a hole in her heart.

Later she would find out that that is the way our Creator made each of us, with a "God shaped hole" in our hearts. Later she would find out that her life was plagued with a human condition that goes all the way back to the beginning of time. Later she would find in her quest for self sufficiency that she had moved away from the One who created her, that she had become separated from God.

This book, a part of a collection called *Spirit Talk* came about through a little girl's personal journey with God, her journey from unbelief into belief, from something that was less-than-life (as God intended it to be for her) to Life that was "very good" in God's eyes.

Very good, in the first two chapters of Genesis, we hear that it was *"in the beginning that God created"* the world, the cosmos, and everything in it, including human beings, and God saw that it was "very good." We also hear that the first couple (Adam and Eve) walked with God, well that is, until they decided to listen to a crafty old serpent instead. The first couple was given, by God, the ability to make choices, and that day by the tree of "Knowledge and of Good and Evil," they made a not so good choice, which spiritually separated them from the One who had created them. Just like the little girl, the first couple found themselves separated from the One who had created them. They made a choice, and people have been making choices every since that day, some good and some not so good.

For example, there was the prodigal son who chose to leave his father. You might have heard the story. In Luke 15:11-24 there were two sons, one who thought it unfair that his father would throw a party for his irresponsible little brother. And another who was called a prodigal.

According to the dictionary, the word "prodigal" means "recklessly wasteful." It is derived from a Latin word, which is translated "to squander." Therefore, a prodigal son is literally a wasteful son, one who throws away opportunities recklessly and wastefully.

The younger son in this famous parable is a waster. He is one of the most famous wasters in the entire Bible. Now, in our imaginations we can read between the lines and pencil in all the sordid ways he must have wasted his inheritance.

He had a good case of the "give-mes." "Give me the share of the property that will belong to me," he said. He takes the money and blows it on "dissolute living." We know this story well. We know all about this prodigal, this waster. And what we don't know, our imaginations are more than happy to provide.

And we know all about the father, too, who takes back his wayward son even before the confession gets completely confessed. The father runs across the field and smothers his son with hugs, a robe, a ring, and a huge party. But, we have to ask ourselves: Why did the prodigal come back?

Well, he began to feel that emptiness in his heart. He knew that something was missing. He realized that he needed that relationship with his father. The scriptures tell us: *"He came to himself."* You know, it's just a fact that God created us for a living relationship with Him (our heavenly Father). And no matter how much we acquire, or how much we achieve, nothing (can replace that personal relationship with God) nothing can satisfy our soul, nothing, not money, or sex, or power, nothing. God knows that.

Have you ever noticed that the central theme of the Bible is the story of God calling us back into that relationship with Him? It is. Jesus called people to accept the relationship God offers them. In Matthew 11:28 we hear Him saying: *Come to Me, all you who are weary and are carrying heavy burdens, and I will give you rest.*

You see, God offers to us, not a system of rules, but a personal relationship with Him. And with that relationship comes a mysterious and wonderful grace, justifying grace, which begins to work the moment we say "yes" to God. And, our acceptance changes everything. In the story of the prodigal, justifying grace begins when the younger brother turns away from his misery and returns home.

Luke 15: 20-24 says: *So he set off and went to his father. But while he was still far off, his father saw him and was filled with compassion; he ran and put his arms around him and kissed him. And the father said in His joy get the fatted calf and kill it, and let us eat and celebrate; for this son of mine was dead and is alive again; he was lost and is found! And they began to celebrate.* His broken relationship with his father was amazingly restored. And that's what it is like for those of us who believe (but it is even better). Through, belief in Jesus Christ, we are restored to an Eternal relationship with God.

Using the analogy of human courtship, when we accept God's grace, we say "yes" to the One who has been wooing and pursuing us. And as in courtship, saying "yes" changes the nature of the relationship completely. For a husband and wife, saying "yes" marks the beginning point of a lifelong commitment to marriage and a shared life. And this commitment (is meant by God) to resemble our eternal commitment to Jesus Christ and His mission.

But, even though a person responds in faith, it can only be done because of God's grace. The apostle Paul confirms that as he writes in Ephesians 2:8-9: *For by grace you have been saved through faith, and this is not your own doing; it is the gift of God -- not the result of works, so that no one may boast. It is only by grace that you have been saved through faith.*

Another interesting fact about salvation is this. It is instantaneous and continuous (all at the same time). It is correct to say: *I was saved* by grace, *I am saved* by grace, and *I will be saved* by grace. In scripture, this spiritual experience of justifying grace is known by several names: salvation, healing, conversion, having one's sins forgiven, or being born again.

And now, as Paul Harvey would say: Here's the rest of the story. The little girl I was telling you about earlier, the one who thought church, was just for children, the one who was on a self sufficient quest for happiness, well that little girl was me. You see, I had chosen the path, the wide path that taught: This life is all there is and you are in charge of making it good. I truly believed that this life was my only chance for happiness. And in my misguided understandings I assumed that after this earthly life, a person just simply ceased to exist.

And because of my childhood experience as a church "drop-off kid," I really didn't even believe that there was a God. And of course if I didn't believe there was a God why in the world would I believe that there was a Heaven or a Hell? It just didn't make sense to me. And so, when you think about all of that, well, it's really not surprising that I didn't come into a saving relationship with Jesus Christ as a child or even as a young adult. The most amazing thing though, is this: God waited patiently, He waited for forty years, for my heart to be ready for the miraculous change that He had in store for His little girl.

I remember it well. I was sitting at the desk in the game room of our 4200 square foot home. And I was feeling that empty feeling in my heart. And I began to pray, really pray, for the first time in my life, I began to pray as though there might just possibly be someone out there to hear me.

I begin by praying: God, if You are really out there, and at that moment God brought back to my memory a verse of scripture that I had learned as a child. It was the verse in Matthew where Jesus says: *Come to Me, all you who are weary and are carrying heavy burdens, and I will give you rest.*

And I said: God, if it is really true that I can have that rest and that peace that Jesus says I can have, I want Him in my heart. I want to give my life to Him. And at that moment my heart was changed.

The way that I saw God, the world around me, other people, and myself was completely different. And as I sat there thinking, I said to myself: Now, I didn't bargain for that. I didn't even know that my heart could or even needed to be changed like that. And then a light bulb came on in my mind.

As the logical thinking person that I am, I realized that I didn't change my heart, but my heart was definitely changed. And I had to ask the question: Well, who did that? If it wasn't me who changed my heart, who did that? Then I realized, that it was something outside of myself that had changed my heart.

And at that moment, I realized that God was real! I began to experience a Joy and Peace and Contentment, like I had never experienced before. I was filled with an unquenchable desire to read the Bible and would do so, two and a half times in the next four months. I also, began to feel a tug on my heart to serve as a pastor in God's church.

Now, I can't tell you that it was easy, no in fact it was quite the opposite, I would say. It was a twelve and a half year journey from call to ordination. But amazingly God was there for me the whole way, strengthening me, encouraging me and carrying me when need be.

And to make a long story short: This *Spirit Talk* collection of books is one small part of my journey with God, one that I wanted to share with you, in hopes that the Lord will take my small offering, multiply it and use it for His glory. And so, here goes. Following you will find a collection of messages that were preached in Chappell Hill, Texas during the second half of 2008. It is my prayer that you might be able to glean a little nugget of God's grace and peace as you incorporate these messages into your walk with Him.

Blessings,
Paula Behrens

True Freedom

Matthew 11:25-30
At that time Jesus said, "I thank you, Father, Lord of heaven and earth, because you have hidden these things from the wise and the intelligent and have revealed them to infants;
yes, Father, for such was your gracious will. All things have been handed over to me by my Father; and no one knows the Son except the Father, and no one knows the Father except the Son and anyone to whom the Son chooses to reveal him. "Come to me, all you that are weary and are carrying heavy burdens, and I will give you rest. Take my yoke upon you, and learn from me; for I am gentle and humble in heart, and you will find rest for your souls. For my yoke is easy, and my burden is light."

Did you hear the story about a little boy who was out helping his dad with the yard work? His dad had asked him to pick up the rocks in a certain area of the yard. After a while he looked over and saw the little boy struggling to pull up a huge rock buried in the dirt. The little boy struggled and struggled while his father watched. Finally, the boy gave up and said: "I can't do it." And his dad asked: "Did you use all of your strength?" And the little boy looked hurt and said: "Yes, sir. I used every ounce of strength I have." And the father smiled and said: "No you didn't. You didn't ask me to help." Then the father walked over and the two of them pulled that big rock out of the dirt together.[1]

This weekend, America has been celebrating freedom. And so, it only seems fitting that we talk about freedom today. And you may be wondering what this story about a little boy and a big rock has to do with freedom. Well, one of the greatest Biblical truths is that true freedom comes only when we choose to be yoked together with Another.

Let us pray: May the words of my mouth and the meditations of each of our hearts be acceptable in Your sight, O God, our Rock and our Redeemer. Amen.

Jesus said: *"I thank you Father, Lord of heaven and earth, because you have hidden these things from the wise and the intelligent and have revealed them to infants."*[2] Jesus was overjoyed, one day, because some had received the good news. *"These little ones,"* these infants, these babes in scribal wisdom had believed the gospel, He proclaimed. Now these people were just like us. God had given them a mind; God had given them the capability and the capacity to think and to reason for themselves. And God had given them a certain amount of self-confidence, as well. These were good things that God had given them. But in order to experience that deeper joy, a joy that goes "soul" deep, and in order to experience the freedom they longed for, they had to combine their human capabilities with something else. They had to be yoked together, with Jesus Christ.

In the early church, we hear that some were astonished at the wisdom of the disciples. Luke tells us: *When the rulers, elders, and scribes in Jerusalem saw the boldness of Peter and John and realized that they were uneducated and ordinary men, they were amazed.*[3] But even though they were uneducated and ordinary, Jesus Himself gave them little slack. He asked tough questions like: *"Who do you say that I am?"* To which Peter replied: *"You are the Messiah, the Son of the living God."*

Peter's knowledge came not through human reason but as a gift of divine revelation. You see, God had met Peter right where he was and gave him divine wisdom just when he needed it. Now, meeting a person right where they are is not an uncommon occurrence in the Bible. In the Gospel of Luke we hear how Christ meets two of the early disciples on a road to Emmaus.

Two of them are walking the familiar road that leads away from Jerusalem, away from the place where Jesus had only days earlier been crucified. But the strange thing is that it is not until Jesus sits at the table with them, *"takes the bread, blesses it, breaks it and gives it to them that their eyes are opened"* to God's presence. It is in the breaking of the bread that they experience Christ.

You know, we too, can experience the presence of Christ as we yield our self to Him, even today. In the breaking of the bread, through prayer, in worship, through everyday experiences, in joy and in sorrow, we can know that it is God's plan that we meet Him on the dusty roads of this life. And as the scriptures are opened to us, as the bread is broken, we begin to understand the key to freedom.

But there are so many things that can distract us; there are so many things, in this life, that can take away our freedom. One writer said: People, today, are in constant danger of becoming enslaved by the very things that are supposed to make life more convenient. Laptop computers, fax machines, pagers and cell phones threaten to take us hostage he said. No matter where we go, our work goes with us. In truth, our time and our life is not our own. Even if we could break free of the ever-encroaching demands of a career, our other responsibilities are enough to occupy our every waking moment, things like volunteer work, civic duties and family responsibilities. We need to spend quality time with our children. We need to be both physically and emotionally present for our spouse. We need to take care of the yard and the cars. We need to balance the checkbook. We need, we need, we need; the list seems endless.

But, somewhere in our hectic schedules we must find time to, maintain a quality devotional life, time to read for personal and spiritual development. Busyness is addictive and it's hard to regain control of our life once we've yielded to it. It's no wonder many of us are tempted to throw up our hands in despair, at least, every once in a while, one author writes.[4]

But there is a solution, I think. There is a way out. The key is to decide to take control of our schedules. And we can begin to do that when we ask this one very important question: Are we going to allow the external pressures of this earthly life to control our schedules or will we allow the witness of the Holy Spirit within us, to set our agendas?

As you consider your list of things you need to do today, I want you to try this. Try dividing them into these four categories. Things that are: Absolutely essential, important but not essential, helpful but not necessary and trivial. Then eliminate all but the first two categories: Those things that are absolutely essential and those things that are very important to you and hopefully to God.

You know, it's God's will that we get rid of the trivial things in our lives, the things that only clutter up our thinking, that take us away from Him and from our loved ones. It is God's desire that we remove from our lives, the things that keep us from making an innocent childlike commitment to Christ.

Now, you may be thinking: I've got so much to do, how can I ever make time for a commitment to anything? Well, listen to this story. One day there was a man who challenged a friend to an all-day wood chopping contest. The challenger worked very hard, stopping only for a brief lunch break. The other man had a leisurely lunch and took several breaks during the day. At the end of the day, the challenger was surprised and annoyed to find that the other fellow had chopped substantially more wood than he had. "I don't get it," he said. "Every time I checked, you were taking a rest, yet you chopped more wood than I did." "But you didn't notice," said the winning woodsman, "that I was sharpening my ax when I sat down to rest."[5]

Being yoked with Christ, daily, gives us the time we need to rest and to sharpen our axe. It gives us the opportunity to prioritize our days, doing away with the unnecessary things and then giving the more difficult things to the Lord. That's the key to *"not growing weary"* in our walk with God.

Growing weary is the consequence of many experiences: We can become weary of waiting. We can become weary of studying and learning. We can become weary of fighting the enemy. We can become weary of criticism and persecution. You see, there are lots of things in life that can cause us to become weary, and if we are not careful, weariness can cut our feet right out from under us. Even so, we need to understand that God doesn't prescribe strength, like a doctor writes a prescription. He doesn't administer energy pills to pop in our mouth. God doesn't give us a quick fix for our moments of weariness.[6] But instead, God promises Himself as our yokemate, everyday, all the time.

Jesus says: *"Come to Me all who are weary and are carrying heavy burdens and I will give you rest. Take My yoke upon you and learn from Me, and you will find rest for your soul."* He says, I am your Greater Strength. You won't be able to move that big rock all by yourself, but if you make a commitment to Me, then you will find the key to overcoming weariness. You will find that with your new God-focused and uncluttered life, comes rest for your soul.

And so, as we come to the Lord's Table today, let each of us examine our hearts, and ask ourselves truthfully, if we have made that necessary, child-like commitment to our Lord. And if you find that you haven't done that. If you find that you are still struggling with weariness in this life, then now is your chance, now is your chance to find the rest and true freedom your soul has been longing for. So be it. Amen.

The Sower... the Seed & the Soil

Matthew 13:1-9, 18-23
That same day Jesus went out of the house and sat beside the sea.
Such great crowds gathered around him that he got into a boat
and sat there, while the whole crowd stood on the beach. And he
told them many things in parables, saying: "Listen! A sower went
out to sow. And as he sowed, some seeds fell on the path, and the
birds came and ate them up. Other seeds fell on rocky ground,
where they did not have much soil, and they sprang up quickly,
since they had no depth of soil. But when the sun rose, they were
scorched; and since they had no root, they withered away. Other
seeds fell among thorns, and the thorns grew up and choked them.
Other seeds fell on good soil and brought forth grain, some a
hundredfold, some sixty, some thirty. Let anyone with ears listen!"

"Hear then the parable of the sower. When anyone hears the word
of the kingdom and does not understand it, the evil one comes and
snatches away what is sown in the heart; this is what was sown on
the path. As for what was sown on rocky ground, this is the one
who hears the word and immediately receives it with joy; yet such
a person has no root, but endures only for a while, and when
trouble or persecution arises on account of the word, that person
immediately falls away. As for what was sown among thorns, this
is the one who hears the word, but the cares of the world and the
lure of wealth choke the word, and it yields nothing. But as for
what was sown on good soil, this is the one who hears the word
and understands it, who indeed bears fruit and yields, in one case a
hundredfold, in another sixty, and in another thirty."

There is a story about an old man who always had witty and wise answers for people who asked him anything. Once, a disrespectful man came to him with his hands covering something he was holding. He told the wise man that he had a small, newly hatched bird in his hands. He challenged the old man to tell him whether the bird was alive or dead. He of course, planned to prove the old man wrong, because if he said the bird was dead, he would simply open his hands to expose a perfectly healthy baby bird. But if he said the bird was alive, then he would crush the bird before opening his hands. But, the old man proved wiser than the disrespectful man thought, because he said: "The bird is whatever you choose him to be."[7] Like the bird in a persons' hand, what the Kingdom of God will be in a person's heart, alive or dead, is dependent upon whatever that person chooses it to be.

Let us pray: May the words of my mouth and the meditations of each of our hearts be acceptable in Your sight, O God, our Rock and our Redeemer. Amen.

In our scripture reading today, we hear Jesus speak about a sower who sows seed on various kinds of soil. The seed that fell along the path could not penetrate the hard earth and so it was picked up by birds and eaten. Our hearts can become hard like that pathway, where the seed has no chance at all of penetrating the dirt. And so Satan, like a bird, swoops down and easily takes it away. Other seed falls on rocky soil, Jesus says, meaning that the soil is thin and beneath it is a layer of limestone which prevents the seed from sinking down deep roots. Therefore the seed that springs up soon dies for lack of roots. If we're not careful, a layer of limestone, can buildup just below the surface of our lives. That can happen if we choose to listen to something other than God, something that can weaken our faith in Him. Or if the layer of limestone doesn't get us, then there are the cares of this world and the deceitfulness of riches that threaten to choke out the word, like the seed that fell among thorns, and thus yielded very little fruit.

But the good, deep soil the soil free of thorns produces a bountiful harvest. Jesus likens the good soil to a person who *"hears the Word and understands it"* or takes it to heart. Now, "understanding" in this passage refers not to an intellectual awareness but to a moral commitment involving one's inmost being; that's what taking God's Word to heart means.

The writer of Matthew conveys to us that there is a difference between simply "hearing" and hearing with "understanding." The person who hears and understands has allowed God's word to sink deep into the depths of their soul, like the seed that fell upon the good soil.

But, sometimes appearances can be deceitful. While studying in the Holy Lands, a seminary professor once met a man who claimed to have memorized the Old Testament, in Hebrew. Needless to say, the astonished professor asked for a demonstration: "Where shall we begin" asked the man? "Psalm 1," replied the professor. So beginning with Psalm 1, the man began to recite from memory, while the professor followed along in his own Hebrew Bible. For two hours the man continued word for word without a mistake as the professor sat in stunned silence. When the demonstration was over, the professor discovered something even more astonishing about the man, he was an atheist.[8] Sometimes appearances can be misleading. In this case, this man's heart had become hardened and closed to the very word he could recite by memory. There is a difference between merely hearing the word and hearing with understanding.

You know, God does not determine who will hear and be receptive to His word and who will not. We are all given a choice. Jesus says, *"Let anyone with ears listen."* We all have been given, spiritual ears to hear God's word. The question is: *"Are we listening?"* Or better yet: Do we strive to listen with understanding? Do we strive to take God's Word to heart, all the time? Not just when it is convenient, but all the time? Do we do that?

Remember the Old Testament prophet Elijah and how he was so zealous for the Lord? He had boldly confronted Ahab regarding a coming drought. And he was faithful to God during a long, lonely time of waiting in a ravine. He had laid his own reputation on the line when he prayed for a widow's son to be restored to life. And he had obeyed God's charge to meet Ahab and the false prophets of Baal on Mount Carmel. Elijah was a great prophet of God. Yet, we hear that he fled into the desert. Why? Well, because he felt his life was in danger because of a woman named Jezebel. After all that God had done for him, after God had used his life so powerfully, he fled into the desert. And he even went so far as to plead that God would take his life. He was in a sad state, indeed, because at that point he had stopped listening to God.

But what did God do? Well, He sought him out by way of His messenger, not to scold him, not to punish him, but to supply the rest and the nourishment he would need in that wilderness. And when Elijah was ready to listen again, God helped him to obtain the spiritual understanding he needed. God instructed him to come out of the cave and to *"stand on the mountain"* in His presence. God's first step was to unleash the fury of a *"great and powerful wind."* It was so strong it literally ripped the landscape apart. Remember that? Very large rocks cascaded down the mountain as if they were pebbles. At the same time, the Lord made it very clear to Elijah that He *"was not in the wind."* The Lord followed the storm with an earthquake. But again the Lord made it clear to Elijah that He *"was not in the earthquake."* The Lord followed the wind and the earthquake with a great fire, possibly to remind Elijah of what He had just done on Mount Carmel in response to Elijah's prayer. But again the Lord made it clear that *"He was not in the fire."*

But if God was not in the wind, the earthquake, or the fire, where was He? Well, we are told that God's personal presence appeared as *"a gentle whisper"* or a quiet rustling. Finally, Elijah was able to listen again with understanding. And at that point God assured him that he was not alone and promptly sent him on his way to continue His work.

Jesus says to us today: *"Are you listening?"* That's something I have to ask myself daily. And really, it's not a bad thing to ask. In fact it's a good thing to ask. Are you listening? And not only that, but it is good to ask for godly wisdom, for understanding, as you listen. The first disciples knew the importance of listening with understanding when they asked: *"Why do You speak to these people in parables?"* And basically Jesus replied: These are the ones that the prophet Isaiah spoke of. These are the ones who have hardened their hearts and thus are unreceptive to God's Word. These are the ones who have consciously chosen to reject Me, Jesus said. They have chosen to reject God's message of good news for them. But as for you, right now, your eyes are blessed because they see and your ears are blessed because they are open and receptive and eager to hear and to learn. And because of that, the seed that was sown there among you has found *"good soil"* and will yield a great harvest for God, some even a hundred-fold.

The amazing thing is that, Jesus doesn't say two-fold, six-fold, or eight-fold, but one hundred-fold. That is how God blesses those whose hearts are prepared for a spiritual harvest. So, with this glorious prospect in mind, that the Word of God can yield one hundred-fold in our lives, let us do all that we can to be open to God's promptings every day, all the time.

You see, it is not good enough to just have been open: At the time of your confirmation, or at the time when you used to teach Sunday school, or the time when you attended church as a child. We need to be continuously open like a cultivated garden. For, where there is "real openness, real listening with understanding", there will be fruits of faith and a great harvest for the Divine Reaper, when He comes to gather in the last days.

Think about this. In the parable there are three things: The Sower (God who is Good) the Seed (God's Word which is Good) and the Soil (the condition of our hearts, which can vary). It is only the third one (the condition of our hearts) that we have any control over.

The apostle Paul wrote: *"Faith comes by hearing, and hearing by the Word of God."*[9] Now, there will probably be times when you question your faith like the great prophet Elijah did. But always remember this. God can rekindle your faith. By listening to God's Word and also striving to hear with understanding, God's Kingdom will have the opportunity to take root and spring up, and bring with it an even greater faith in God, and His purpose for your life.

But, we each have a choice. Our hearts can be a sterile pathway, a stony plateau, a thorn-covered thicket, or a well-cultivated garden filled with rich fertile soil. We have a choice about whether the kingdom of God will live or die in our lives. We can choose to open up our hearts and let it flourish, or we can crush it, like the man with the little fledgling bird.

You know, God has great plans for our lives. And so I hope we will always be open to the growth of God's Kingdom. If you've already done that, opened your heart to God's Kingdom work, and if you choose to continue doing that, then Jesus would say that your heart is like the "good soil," which will bear "fruit," up to a hundred-fold in this life, and even into eternity. Amen.

A Hidden Treasure

Matthew 13:31-32; 44-52

He put before them another parable: "The kingdom of heaven is like a mustard seed that someone took and sowed in his field; it is the smallest of all the seeds, but when it has grown it is the greatest of shrubs and becomes a tree, so that the birds of the air come and make nests in its branches."

"The kingdom of heaven is like treasure hidden in a field, which someone found and hid; then in his joy he goes and sells all that he has and buys that field. "Again, the kingdom of heaven is like a merchant in search of fine pearls; on finding one pearl of great value, he went and sold all that he had and bought it. "Again, the kingdom of heaven is like a net that was thrown into the sea and caught fish of every kind; when it was full, they drew it ashore, sat down, and put the good into baskets but threw out the bad. So it will be at the end of the age. The angels will come out and separate the evil from the righteous and throw them into the furnace of fire, where there will be weeping and gnashing of teeth. "Have you understood all this?" They answered, "Yes." And he said to them, "Therefore every scribe who has been trained for the kingdom of heaven is like the master of a household who brings out of his treasure what is new and what is old."

A young man went to an old desert monk and asked: Why is it that so many people come out to the desert to seek God and yet most of them give up after a short time and return to their lives in the city?

The old monk told him, "Yesterday evening my dog saw a rabbit running for cover and he began to chase the rabbit, barking loudly. Soon other dogs joined in the chase, barking and running. They ran a great distance and alerted many other dogs. Soon the wilderness was echoing the sounds of their pursuit but the chase went on into the night. After a little while, many of the dogs grew tired and dropped out. A few chased the rabbit until the night was almost over. But by morning, only my dog continued the hunt. Do you know why," asked the monk. "No," replied the young man, "please tell me." "It is simple," said the desert father. "My dog was the only one who had caught a glimpse of the rabbit in the first place."[10]

Jesus told a parable about a man who one day "caught a glimpse of" a great treasure in a field. And because he understood the value of the treasure, he sacrificed everything to receive it.

Let us pray: May the words of my mouth and the meditations of each of our hearts be acceptable in Your sight, O God, our Rock and our Redeemer. Amen.

Jesus said: *"The kingdom of heaven is like treasure hidden in a field, which someone found and hid; then in his joy he goes and sells all that he has and buys that field."*[11] The treasure that this man had found meant so much to him that he sold everything he had to receive it. That's what the kingdom of heaven is like. When Jesus spoke of the kingdom of heaven, He was talking about the rule of God in the lives of people and in the world. And we learn that it is not only a future event, but also, a present event, as it can already be found deep within a persons' heart and among the community of believers.

Let me share with you a few truths about this great treasure. First, the treasure of God's kingdom creates life's greatest joy. For the man who "caught a glimpse" of that hidden treasure, it was the greatest discovery he had ever made. And it filled his life with joy. That's what the kingdom of heaven is like, life's greatest joy.

Everybody wants to find joy. Not everybody is finding it, though. A while back there was a song called, "*Looking for love in all the wrong places.*" Many people are looking for happiness and joy and love in all the wrong places, still. They would like to be happy, but they cannot define it. They would love to find joy, but they don't know where it is. They long to find Love, but they don't know how to go about it. So they wander through life like "*sheep without a shepherd*" in a wilderness.

This is not anything new; it goes all the way back to Jesus' time; He talked about people being "*like sheep without a shepherd.*" Now, sometimes these things, happiness, joy and love are seen as tangible things, things we can get, or buy, or purchase somehow. But what we don't realize is that these things are byproducts, they are the results of something else. Happiness, joy and love are not found in the things we possess, but in what possesses us. They are not found in what we can own, but in Who owns us. They are not found in what we create for ourselves, but in what we discover has been there all along, like a treasure hidden in a field.

C. S. Lewis wrote a book called <u>Surprised By Joy</u>. Joy is always a great discovery, a great surprise. I know firsthand about that. For years, I thought I could find happiness in tangible things like: work, family, cars, a home, and computers. But, finally, when I least expected it God surprised me with His divine joy, like a treasure buried in a field. But, it wasn't visible to me until I begin to feel this emptiness inside, until I realized that I had shut the door on God in my life. The treasure of His kingdom wasn't visible to me until I realized that I needed to open that door from the inside of my heart. You see, Christ had been knocking for a long time, but I had been ignoring Him. It was sort of like a game show to me. Maybe, the things I needed could be found behind door #1 or door #2 or door #3. Surely, it wasn't behind the door marked Jesus Christ.

But, I was wrong. For many years I was wrong. It wasn't until I opened the door marked Jesus Christ that I realized that the Ultimate joy is only found in our citizenship in God's kingdom rule. It is only there that we find our sense of well-being, purpose and fulfillment. Only in God's kingdom rule do we find the answers for life's questions. When we make that discovery, God's Kingdom rule begins to fill our lives with joy, that can't help but spill over into all areas of our life.

First, the treasure of God's kingdom creates life's greatest joy. And second, it costs life's highest price. The greatest joy is not free. It requires something. We hear that the man in the parable *"sold all that he had."* And he did it willingly. He sold all that he had in order to raise enough money to receive the field in which the treasure was hidden. The kingdom of Heaven is like that. It costs life's highest price.

Now, that might sound bad to you. But think about this. There are many things, many bad things that will cost you everything. And when those things are through with you they will leave you broken and in need of God's healing grace. For example, alcohol, in and of itself is not a bad thing. Jesus once changed water into wine at a wedding feast. And the apostle Paul told Timothy to take a little wine with his water for his health. In and of itself, wine is not a bad thing, but for a person who abuses it, seeking to numb the pain of life instead of dealing with their problems, well, alcohol can be deadly. And then there are drugs. Through the grace of God, modern science is constantly discovering new drugs that can help us to live long and quality lives. But when drugs are abused, lives are destroyed. Then there is something that we see all around us on billboards, in advertisements, at the movies, on Television, human sexuality. It's a healthy part of what it means to be human. Without it our race would become extinct pretty quickly. It's about procreation. And it's also a gift from God given to a man and a woman, to be shared only within the bond of marriage.

The marriage covenant is sort of like a well-built fireplace, I think. You see, a fire can be enjoyed as long as it stays within the walls of the fireplace. But if it gets outside of the fireplace, if it spreads to the middle of the living room, well, it will more than likely destroy the whole house. Like that, sexuality outside the safe confines of the marriage covenant which has been established by God, outside of that covenant, sexuality brings devastation into every life it touches, as well.

You see anything we commit our lives to can wind up costing us everything. What we choose can ultimately cost us everything. And the kingdom of heaven is no different. Jesus did say: *"Those who want to save their life will lose it, and those who lose their life for My sake will find it."* And then He reasoned: *"For what will it profit them if they gain the whole world but forfeit their life?"* [12]

Yes, the kingdom of heaven will cost us everything if we think of everything in a worldly way. But as we loosen our grip on the things of this world, we discover an amazing thing. We discover that the kingdom begins to take root in our soul and grow. We discover that it creates within us the very best we can be. And, we discover that it calls forth from us the very best we could ever say or do or think. We discover that the kingdom of heaven is Life; it is True Life that grows from within. And that is what God intends for each of us.

A little boy once came home from Sunday school and told his mother that he had learned about inheriting God's kingdom. They had studied what it meant to inherit something. And so he said to his mother, "I'd like my inheritance now, please." And his mother responded: "That's too bad, because, I'm not through with it yet."

In the kingdom of heaven, however, we can have a part of our inheritance now. The apostle Paul writes: *The Spirit Himself bears witness with our spirit that we are children of God, now and if children, then heirs, heirs of God and joint heirs with Christ.*[13] The treasure of God's kingdom will be given to those who make a decision for Christ, turning control of their lives over to Him.

First, the treasure of God's kingdom creates life's greatest joy. Second the treasure of Gods kingdom will cost us our life. And third, the treasure of God's kingdom calls for a deep commitment. Because the kingdom of Heaven offers us the greatest joy at the highest cost, it calls for the deepest commitment, as well. Jesus said that the man sold *"all he had"* in order to raise enough money to receive *"the field where the treasure was hidden."* In other words, this man made the commitment. He bought it. He followed through with it all the way.

Now, why did Jesus tell this parable? Well, I think He told this parable so as to train His disciples about the sacrifice that would be required of them. The greatest treasure, God's kingdom rule, calls for sacrifice. It calls for taking a chance. It calls for living on the edge for God, which may include many things, like the way you raise your children, like the way you sacrificially serve your spouse, like the way you take care of an aging parent, or the way you reach out to a stranger with the love of Christ, just to name a few. All of these things are signs that a person has the treasure of God's Kingdom in his or her heart.

There was a man in Florida who used to wrestle with alligators. And one time after one of his performances a lady noticed he was wearing a string of alligator teeth around his neck. She said, "Oh that is sort of like wearing a string of pearls." And he replied, "Not quite, lady. Anyone can open an oyster."

Likewise, anyone can be religious on the outside. But having the treasure of God's kingdom in your heart is something else, altogether. Being religious on the outside, means thinking that Jesus was merely a good teacher and that the Bible, well, is just like any other book, written for our enjoyment. But, if Jesus Christ is only a teacher, and if the Bible is just like any other book, then we are going to be pretty frustrated when we try to reach the standard that is found there for us.

Think about this. Why would God present us with such a lofty ideal if we can't possibly come close to reaching it? For example, why would God tell us to be what we can never be, like being "pure in heart?"[14] And there are so many more that I am not going to name right now. Why would God tell us to follow an example, which in our own human strength, can never be met?

Well, you see, Jesus Christ came to do much more than just teach, He came to make of us what we were created to be. The greatest treasure of God's kingdom is that Jesus Christ can place within anyone the same nature that ruled His own life. That's what having the treasure of God's kingdom within our heart is about. And, it requires commitment. Because the kingdom of heaven offers us the greatest joy at the highest cost, it calls for the deepest commitment, as well.

It calls us to give our lives to Christ. It puts us among the people of God who have been faithful to Him across the centuries. It re-orders our priorities; it re-orders the things we live for. It leads us to dedicate our lives, who we are, what we can do, our abilities, our hopes, and our dreams, to God.

And the good news is that in the midst of this kind of commitment we make the most marvelous discovery. We find that even though we thought the cost was high, we discover suddenly that we have riches untold, that we have riches beyond measure as we are overwhelmed by the value of the treasure we have discovered.

The greatest good news for us is that we can have all we want of God's treasure; we can have all we are willing to receive. And when we do receive God's treasure, my goodness, we find that it is the Discovery of a lifetime.

Have you "caught a glimpse" of God's kingdom? I hope so. Because if you have caught a glimpse, then I know that you will never want to give up until you receive it in all of its fullness. Let's commit to do that today, let us all receive His gift more fully, today and every day. Amen.

In The Boat

Matthew 14:22-33
Immediately he made the disciples get into the boat and go on ahead to the other side, while he dismissed the crowds. And after he had dismissed the crowds, he went up the mountain by himself to pray. When evening came, he was there alone, but by this time the boat, battered by the waves, was far from the land, for the wind was against them. And early in the morning he came walking toward them on the sea. But when the disciples saw him walking on the sea, they were terrified, saying, "It is a ghost!" And they cried out in fear. But immediately Jesus spoke to them and said, "Take heart, it is I; do not be afraid." Peter answered him, "Lord, if it is you, command me to come to you on the water." He said, "Come." So Peter got out of the boat, started walking on the water, and came toward Jesus. But when he noticed the strong wind, he became frightened, and beginning to sink, he cried out, "Lord, save me!" Jesus immediately reached out his hand and caught him, saying to him, "You of little faith, why did you doubt?" When they got into the boat, the wind ceased. And those in the boat worshiped him, saying, "Truly you are the Son of God."

Dr. Will Willimon tells of a visit he made one afternoon to the office of a lawyer who was a member of his church. He says: It was at the end of the day. I entered his law firm. Everyone had left. All was dark, except for a light coming from the inner office.

He invited me to come back to his office. "Didn't expect to see you here, preacher," he said in a tired voice. "Come on in, I was just about to fix myself a drink. Can I interest you in one?" "Sure," I said, "if it's caffeine free and diet."

"He poured out the drinks, offered me a seat, leaned back in his chair and put his feet on the disordered desk in front of him. "What sort of day have you had?" I asked. "A typical day," he said, again sounding tired. "Misery, actually."

"Oh, I'm sorry. What was miserable about it?" I asked. "My day began with my assisting of a young man to sue his employer for supposed work related injuries. All legal. Not particularly moral, but legal.

Then, by lunchtime I was helping a client evade his workers' insurance payments. It's legal too. And this afternoon, I have been enabling a woman to ruin her husband's life forever with the sweetest divorce you ever saw. That's my day."

"Which," he said, "helps to explain why I'm in church on Sundays." "It's not the sermons that I come for, preacher," he said sorry, no offense but, "it's the music. I go a whole week sometimes with nothing beautiful or good until Sunday. You see, when I hear that music, it is for me the difference between life and death."

You know, sometimes we feel that way when we finally get the chance to be in God's presence. Why are you here this morning? You don't have to answer that, because, you see, I know that you need this time in God's sanctuary. We all do. We need the songs, we need the music, we need to hear the words spoken from the pulpit or from someone sitting in the pew. We all need this time in God's sanctuary.

This morning our scripture reading is a familiar one. It's the one where Peter gets out of the boat and begins to walk to Jesus on the water. And we will be talking about that, but we will also be talking about something even more important, I think, that of being in God's "Boat."

Let us pray: May the words of my mouth and the meditations of each of our hearts be acceptable in Your sight, O God, our Rock and our Redeemer. Amen.

Jesus has sent the disciples away. He dismisses the crowd. And then He goes off alone to pray. The disciples are in a boat in the midst of a storm. And when Jesus comes to them they don't recognize Him. Superstition rules their lives, yet Peter, for one reason or another recognizes his Lord. Then he takes a chance. He asks the Lord to bid him to come to Him in the middle of the sea.

Now, it must have taken a lot of courage for Peter to do what he did. And I wonder if we would have that same kind of courage. You know, given the choice between continuing in a bad situation or venturing out into the unknown, most people will decide to stay put, to stay where they are: Thus it is that a woman won't seek counseling when she and her children are being abused. Because of fear she refuses to get the help that could bring healing to her family. Thus it is that a man will work for years in a job that is slowly destroying his health and happiness rather than start over in another business. Thus it is that a teenager will not speak to someone who they would really like to get to know because they are afraid of being laughed at or rejected.

Most people suffer from a lack of boldness at some time in their lives. I am sure that we can all add to the list of things we wanted to do but were afraid to take that first frightening step. But you know what? The thing about our Lord is that whether we make the decision to step out in faith or begin to sink in our efforts, He knows where we are. And one way or another, He will be there to encourage us and to lift us out of the stormy waters of life.

A prisoner of war[15] said that only once during his confinement in a labor camp, did he become so discouraged that he thought about suicide. He was outdoors, on a work detail, and he had reached a point where he no longer cared whether he lived or died. When he had a break, he sat down, and a stranger sat beside him, someone he had never seen before and would never see again. For no apparent reason, this stranger took a stick and drew a cross on the ground. The prisoner sat and stared at that cross for a long while. And he later wrote: "Staring at that cross, I realized that therein lies freedom." At that point, because of the cross of Christ, that man found the strength to ride out the storm.[16]

In the midst of a storm, we hear that Peter got out of the boat at the Lord's bidding. But that's not the end of the story. While Peter was trusting in and focusing on Jesus, he did well. But when he began to look at the circumstances that surrounded him, the wind and the waves around him, he began to sink. Do you remember Peter's prayer when he began to sink? It's a very short one. He cried out, "Lord, save me!" I prayed a prayer like that once.

A few years ago, I was on my way to teach a Sunday school class at the church I was attending. It had been storming all night long and I had to drive across town to get to the church. I decided that morning to take the toll road because it was very high and less likely to flood. And as I was driving along I came to a big high ramp that went over other major freeways. Now this was a road that I was used to traveling so I was pretty comfortable with the situation, but I had forgotten that sometimes huge, lake size puddles formed as the rain rushed down the ramps. There was a car in front of me in the lane to the right and I wasn't too far behind. I saw that car hit one of those huge puddles, which blanketed my car with a sheet of water. Now, I had had this happen before, except the water this time was so thick that I couldn't see anything in front of me for what seemed to be an eternity. That's when I prayed a prayer pretty much like Peter's prayer. I said, "Oh God, please help me!"

I can remember thinking, "Okay, I think the road goes straight," but then I thought, "No, I think the road curves to the left." Then I began to doubt and started to think: "This is it, I know I am going over the edge, I'm going to see my Lord today." And I prayed again that short prayer, "Oh, God, please help me!" Then I felt a calmness that said, "Okay, whatever happens, God will be with me." I heard in my mind: "Just hold the steering wheel the same way it was when you went into that lake and lightly pump the brakes." So that's what I did and when I finally came out on the other side I could again see the car in front of me as it went along its merry way, completely oblivious to what had happened to me.

And then I noticed something else that was very unnerving, I noticed that I no longer had a windshield wiper on the driver's side. So I thought: Do I stop on the side of the freeway and risk getting hit from behind or do I go on? And then I figured out that if I leaned over to the passenger's side, I could see the road in front of me. So that's what I did the rest of the way to church. I think that I probably felt a lot like Peter must have felt. I had to stay calm and I had to focus on God's ability to deliver me. I had my moments of doubt but I also knew that God was with me.

Now, I don't know what storms of life will come your way this week, or what storm you may be enduring at this very moment. But I know this: Even as the storm rages around you, if you will listen very carefully, you will hear a gentle voice saying: *"Take heart, it is I; do not be afraid."* And in time the storm will pass. And Jesus will still be there beside you.

Peter had his doubts and he began to sink. But then he remembered from whence his help had always come, and he cried out to the Lord. And Jesus reached out his hand to lift him back up. And this is the part of the story that I find most interesting. Right after He lifted him up, where did Jesus take Peter? Well, He took him right back to the boat to be with the others.

Likewise, in the midst of our storms, God allows us to leave the boat. But He doesn't want us to stay out there in the stormy waters too long. As soon as we possibly can, God's desire is for us to get back into the boat with the others. Why? Because that is where we will find, the support we so desperately need. That is where we will find other people who are riding out similar storms in their lives. It is there in the boat that we learn to covenant together as God's people. And it is there in the boat, with the community of believers that we find Jesus Christ and salvation, as Jesus turns chaos into calmness, and speaks to the storms of our lives, saying: *"Do not fear, it is I."* Do not fear; I am right here beside you to take you back to the safe confines of the boat.

And so this is what I would like us to take away with us this morning. I would like us to take with us the fact that, we are all a part of God's covenant people and that we are all suppose to be in this boat together. Every one of us has a place here, in the boat, with God and with one another.

Jesus told His disciples to get into the boat. And that is what we are to do every week. Show up and get into the boat. Now, one week you may be here to give support, another week you may be here to receive. Or you may not know why you are here sometimes, but that's okay. We don't have to know all the details because God knows them. You see, this is God's boat and God's plan, we just need to make the effort to be here and He will do the rest. Praise God. Amen.

Serving at the Lord's Table

Matthew 14:13-21
Now when Jesus heard this, he withdrew from there in a boat to a deserted place by himself. But when the crowds heard it, they followed him on foot from the towns. When he went ashore, he saw a great crowd; and he had compassion for them and cured their sick. When it was evening, the disciples came to him and said, "This is a deserted place, and the hour is now late; send the crowds away so that they may go into the villages and buy food for themselves." Jesus said to them, "They need not go away; you give them something to eat." They replied, "We have nothing here but five loaves and two fish." And he said, "Bring them here to me." Then he ordered the crowds to sit down on the grass. Taking the five loaves and the two fish, he looked up to heaven, and blessed and broke the loaves, and gave them to the disciples, and the disciples gave them to the crowds. And all ate and were filled; and they took up what was left over of the broken pieces, twelve baskets full. And those who ate were about five thousand men, besides women and children.

A number of years ago a 13 year-old boy read about a missionary's work in another country. And he wanted to help. And he had enough money to buy one bottle of aspirin. He wrote to the Air Force and asked if they could fly over the hospital there and drop the bottle down. A radio station broadcast the story about his concern for helping others. And the response was overwhelming. Eventually the boy was flown by the government to that hospital along with 4 1/2 tons of medical supplies worth $400,000 freely given by thousands of people. And when the missionary heard the story, he said, "I never thought one child could do so much."[17]

Our scripture reading today is about the disciples who didn't have much. But what they did have, they offered to Christ. And thousands of hungry people were fed.

Let us pray: May the words of my mouth and the meditations of each of our hearts be acceptable in Your sight, O God, our Rock and our Redeemer. Amen.

The sermon title today is: "Serving at the Lord's Table." And sometimes we think that means taking a $1,000 check and laying it on the altar and saying: "Here's my life, Lord. I'm giving it all to you" and then I'm walking away. But the truth of the matter is that God wants us to go to the bank and cash that $1,000 check in for quarters. And then we go through life giving away twenty-five cents here, fifty cents there, and so on.

God wants us to be active participants in feeding the people. He wants us to share in what He will do. Instead of watching a ball game, we could spend some time visiting a lonely person in a nursing home. Instead of sipping coffee and reading the newspaper, we could get dressed and go to teach a Bible study. Instead of playing games on the computer or golf or anything else we enjoy, we could listen to a friend tell us about what's going on in their life. Why? Well, because these will be the times when we will feel the grace of God most powerfully, as He works through us, to help another.

Would it surprise you to learn that everything in your life right now is pretty much the way you made it? It's true. You have chosen how you would respond to hundreds of options as they have presented themselves to you in this life. And so do you know what that means? Well, it means that we can choose to learn certain responses. And if we can choose to learn certain responses, it only stands to reason that we can also choose to unlearn them. We have choices, we can choose good habits and helping others or we can choose bad habits and think only of ourselves.

Consider this; consider how hopping fleas are trained. The fleas are put into a glass jar. As they try to jump in the jar, they bump their heads on the lid. And over time, they forget they can jump any higher than the jar. And because of fear of bumping their heads they learn to never go beyond the limits of the jar, even though the lid has been removed. Through continued failure they have become conditioned to confinement.

So it is with us, if we allow it. Our self-made limitations sometimes cause us to forget what our true capacity "in Christ" really is. And we respond like the disciples, saying: *"Well, we only have five small loaves of bread and two fishes."* You see, the disciples were only trusting in their own abilities and not in the abilities of their Lord.

The apostle Paul tells us that there are two elements that need to be present, so as to trust in our Lord. First, he says that we have to *"believe with our heart and second, he says we have to confess with our mouth."* Notice that he doesn't say *"believe with your mind."* Now, certainly believing with our mind is part of believing with our heart. But the reality is that, intellectual faith alone is not enough. To trust in Jesus Christ requires that we embrace Him with our emotions, with our imagination and with our heart.

Pastor Michael tells of the time that his two-year-old nephew first saw snow. The whole family gathered around to witness this momentous event. He said that the boy's eyes grew wide with awe as he saw the sparkling crystals falling from the sky. He quivered at the touch of a snowflake on his face. "His mind was a confusion of strange, conflicting realities: White, cold ... tingling ... melting snow" which caused an overload so great, so overwhelming that he simply fell backward into the drifts.[18]

You see, this little boy had given up trying to understand snow and had given in to merely experiencing the wonder of it. In order to believe that the scriptures are true, in order to believe that Jesus Christ does have the power to perform miracles, just as He multiplied the bread and fishes that day, ultimately, we have to say, I don't understand fully how God does what He does, but I am willing to fall back into the drifts of His miraculous ability to do that which I cannot do alone. That is what, *"believing with ones heart"* is all about.

Also Paul says that we have to *"confess with our mouth."* Strangely enough, for some, talking about Jesus is more difficult than trusting Him. And yet, this is one of the requirements of our faith. We are required to share with others what God has done in our lives.

Now most of us are not going to be great evangelistic preachers. There are only a few "Billy Grahams" in this world. And maybe that is just as well, because this world also needs listeners. There are many people today who just need someone to listen to them. And then, after they have poured out their hearts, wouldn't it be appropriate to ask: "Have you prayed about that?" And wouldn't it be appropriate to say: "When I am down, I have a few scripture verses that give me comfort," and then point them to some of the passages that have helped you? If you don't know exactly where those verses are, well, get your Bible out, look them up, write them down, and carry them with you wherever you go. You just never know when God will use them.

Nobody's asking you to stand on a soap-box or in a pulpit, unless that's your calling. You're only asked to be a good neighbor, be a good friend. Just commit yourself to listening to the doubts and fears of those around you and then remember to, put in a good word for Jesus.

Once there was a little boy who was trying to raise some money by collecting old bottles. He was going door-to-door in his neighborhood. When he came to the home of a woman who was known as the "town grouch," the little boy asked, "Do you have any coke bottles?" "No," she replied with a sour look on her face. Then he said, "Do you have any old whiskey bottles?" "Young man," the woman replied, "Do I look like the type of person who would have old whiskey bottles?" The little boy studied her for a moment and then asked, "Well, do you have any old vinegar bottles?"[19]

Some people, like this woman go through life with a negative attitude, which, you know, is a self-made glass jar. And there are other self-made jars such jars that say to us: You can't do that, it isn't practical. You're not smart enough. It will cost too much. People will laugh at you. You're too young. You're too old. Your health won't allow it. Your parents won't allow it. It will take too long. You don't have the education. And so on, and so forth.

And, sometimes, even Christians get caught in a glass jar. But suppose we could remember that in God's strength, we can remove those jars. If we remembered that, do you think we would still allow our jars to limit us to hopping only just so far and no further? Suppose we became aware of the fact that self-made jars like, resentment, hurt, hate, grudges and greed, are just that, self-imposed, imaginary glass jars that can be removed. Once aware of that fact, we can make changes that will free us from our self-imposed limitations. And finally when those limitations are removed, we will then be ready and able to serve more effectively at the Lord's Table.

You know, the disciples, in this story are not portrayed in a very positive light when Jesus says to them: "You give them something to eat." And they respond by saying: "What?" "Impossible, only the best caterers, with tons of food and plenty of notice, could feed a crowd like this."

Why do you think the disciples responded in this way? Well, because they must have thought that the little bit they had would never be enough. But they were wrong, because, little is always much when Jesus is involved. He took the little bit they brought, *"looked up to heaven, blessed and broke the loaves, and gave them back to the disciples."* In turn the disciples served the food to the crowd and you know the rest of the story.

In the opening scene of that famous movie *The Wizard of Oz,* we see Dorothy in Kansas, and everything is in black-and-white. Remember that? Then, a tornado blows her and Toto and her house "somewhere over the rainbow," and she opens the door on Oz, and suddenly everything is in color. Now, if you can imagine that, then you have a good mental picture of what Jesus does for us when we make the decision to place our lives and what little bit we have in His capable hands. And as we faithfully and trustingly offer our resources to Him, our eyes are opened, and we finally realize just how powerful He is, to multiply our gifts and our graces all for His glory.

And, you know what?   We don't have to have great and unusual talents, or we don't have to have millions of dollars to make a difference for God. Remember the little boy with the bottle of aspirin? He only had one bottle.

This morning I would like to urge each of us, to think about what it would be like to give whatever we have for God's use, giving whatever we have, and then leaving the results to God.

And in that light, I also invite you to ask yourself these questions: What gifts and graces do I have that I'm not fully activating for God? And, at what table, does He want me to serve? You know, God does have a special place just for you, in His serving line. Amen.

Worthy Is The Lamb

Revelation 5:1-14

Then I saw in the right hand of the one seated on the throne a scroll written on the inside and on the back, sealed with seven seals; and I saw a mighty angel proclaiming with a loud voice, "Who is worthy to open the scroll and break its seals?" And no one in heaven or on earth or under the earth was able to open the scroll or to look into it. And I began to weep bitterly because no one was found worthy to open the scroll or to look into it. Then one of the elders said to me, "Do not weep. See, the Lion of the tribe of Judah, the Root of David, has conquered, so that he can open the scroll and its seven seals." Then I saw between the throne and the four living creatures and among the elders a Lamb standing as if it had been slaughtered, having seven horns and seven eyes, which are the seven spirits of God sent out into all the earth. He went and took the scroll from the right hand of the one who was seated on the throne. When he had taken the scroll, the four living creatures and the twenty-four elders fell before the Lamb, each holding a harp and golden bowls full of incense, which are the prayers of the saints. They sing a new song: "You are worthy to take the scroll and to open its seals, for you were slaughtered and by your blood you ransomed for God saints from every tribe and language and people and nation; you have made them to be a kingdom and priests serving our God, and they will reign on earth." Then I looked, and I heard the voice of many angels surrounding the throne and the living creatures and the elders; they numbered myriads of myriads and thousands of thousands, singing with full voice, "Worthy is the Lamb that was slaughtered to receive power and wealth and wisdom and might and honor and glory and blessing!" Then I heard every creature in heaven and on earth and under the earth and in the sea, and all that is in them, singing, "To the one seated on the throne and to the Lamb be blessing and honor and glory and might forever and ever!" And the four living creatures said, "Amen!" And the elders fell down and worshiped.

In a column in The San Francisco Chronicle children were once asked this question: "What does God look like?" And one child wrote, "Jesus and God both have a circle over their heads. They try to walk careful and stay right underneath it because it lights up. They live in heaven. Sometimes God comes here but most of the time He stays up high. In church He stays way in the top part." Another child wrote, "God wears a nightgown and shoes like you wear at the beach and He's tall. He never goes to sleep because at night everybody's asking Him to watch so they'll be all right." And a four-year-old wrote, "Sometimes you can kind of see God when you look way up at the trees. You can kind of see a face. It looks like a face. Maybe it's Him."[20] Many of us, as children, had misconceptions about God. But as we've grown in our faith, as we come into His sanctuary week after week, and as we've paid attention to the ways God has been known to move and work in our world, hopefully, we've gained a little more insight about Him.

One person asked the question: Why is it that people faithfully come into God's sanctuary week after week? And then he deliberately studied this phenomena deciding that most people come to church because they want to experience God. And, I think that's true. We do want to see God, we want to touch Him and feel His presence. We love experiencing fellowship with other believers, we love singing the songs of faith, but most of all we are hungry for an experience of transcendence.

Let us pray: May the words of my mouth and the meditations of each of our hearts be acceptable in Your sight, O God, our Rock and our Redeemer. Amen.

Today's message is about touching God. Today we are going to try and seek out how we human beings, with our feeble senses, can possibly experience the Almighty.

We will begin with a passage from the book of Revelation, the book that seeks to usher us into the presence of God. The passage is about Jesus, and we hear John saying: *Then I looked, and I heard the voice of many angels surrounding the throne and the living creatures and the elders; they numbered myriads of myriads and thousands of thousands, singing with full voice, "Worthy is the Lamb that was slaughtered to receive power and wealth and wisdom and might and honor and glory and blessing!" Then I heard every creature in heaven and on earth and under the earth and in the sea, and all that is in them, singing, "To the one seated on the throne and to the Lamb be blessing and honor and glory and might forever and ever!" And the four living creatures said, "Amen!" And the elders fell down and worshiped. "Worthy is the Lamb."* I think that's a good place to begin.

Touching God begins with the Lamb of God, Jesus. And for a Christian there is no other way to approach God. We cannot reach Him with our reasoning. We cannot see Him or find Him with our telescopes. We cannot hear Him with sensitive listening devices. All we can know about God is what God chooses to reveal to us and, as Christians, we believe that God chose to reveal Himself through the life of one person, Jesus of Nazareth.

Now, that may sound a little narrow-minded to some. But, think about this. Years ago there was a pastor who had a fascinating way of approaching the subject of Truth with confirmation students. He did that by starting each class with a jar full of beans. At the beginning of the class he would ask his students to guess how many beans were in the jar, and then he wrote down their guesses on a big pad of paper. Then he helped them make a list of their favorite songs. When both lists were complete he revealed the actual number of beans in the jar. The whole class looked over their guesses, to see whose estimate was closest to being right.

Then the pastor turned to their list of favorite songs, asking: "And which one of these songs is closest to being right?" And, of course, the students always thought that that was a strange question, because, really a person's favorite song is strictly a matter of taste, isn't it? Then the pastor would say: "Okay, when you decide what to believe when it comes to your faith, would that be more like guessing the number of beans in the jar, or would it, be more like choosing your favorite song?" And the students would always answer: Choosing your faith is more like choosing your favorite song, it's a matter of taste.[21]

But, is it really? Is our faith just a matter of taste, or is there an absolute standard by which we can judge our beliefs, just as we can measure how many beans there are in a jar? For those of us who follow Jesus, there is an absolute standard for our faith. And it's a good thing too. Because, you see, in our world today, without Jesus we could believe all kinds of strange things about God.

Now, I do respect the importance of other world religions because I believe that God can and does work in the lives of people in different ways. I believe that God does work in the lives of all who earnestly seek out the Truth. After all, Jesus did say: *Ask, and it will be given you; seek, and you will find; knock, and the door will be opened for you. For everyone who asks receives, and everyone who searches finds, and for everyone who knocks, the door will be opened.*[22]

Bruce Melver in his book, Just as Long as I'm Riding up Front, tells a wonderful story about a little girl named Emily. Emily's parents were graduates of Baylor University. And like most Baylor grads they were avid, supporters of the "Baylor Bears." Emily had attended Baylor University football games ever since she was a toddler. And when she was three years old, Emily came home one day from Sunday school, sat down in her little chair, and volunteered to sing a "new song." It went like this.

Zacchaeus was a wee little man, a wee little man was he; He climbed up in a sycamore tree, the Savior for to see. And when the Savior came that way, He looked up in the tree and said, Sic 'em, Bears![23]

Now, it is true that an attitude like that is okay when rooting for your favorite sports team, but it's not so good when it comes to how we should be, in regards to our faith as Christians. Because, you see, if a person is earnestly seeking God, I believe that no matter how their path begins, if they are earnestly seeking God, He will open a door for them to lead them to Himself.

You know, without Jesus, even we Christians might believe all kinds of strange things about God. For example, without Jesus we could believe that God wants us to kill people in His name. That is what some people believe. They think that if you believe differently than them, then your life is worthless. There have been fanatics in almost every religion. But we, you and I who are seeking the Truth, know that that mentality is not from God as we hear Jesus words: *You have heard that it was said, "You shall love your neighbor and hate your enemy." But I say to you, Love your enemies and pray for those who persecute you, so that you may be children of your Father in heaven."*[24]

Here's another example of wrong thinking. Without Jesus we might believe that God is cruel and vengeful and wreaks havoc on people's lives for no apparent reason. But then, we hear Jesus saying about God the Father: *"He makes His sun rise on the evil and on the good, and sends rain on the righteous and on the unrighteous."*[25] Our God is not cruel; our God is not vengeful and even though there are consequences that come about because we live in a fallen world, our God is a God who desires wholeness for all people and for His creation. Without Jesus we are free to believe all kinds of strange things about God. Without Jesus we can easily fall into error. Without Jesus we would have no model for abundant living because we would have no one to inspire us to be our best.

Lance Armstrong, a famous bicyclist, didn't become a five-time winner of the *Tour de France* without having a major competitive streak. Armstrong was a competitive and disciplined athlete, and he admitted that he had a hard time losing. When he won a bronze medal at the 2000 Olympics in Sydney, Australia, Armstrong appeared to have lost the higher medals with dignity. Privately, however, he went into a period of deep depression. One day, his wife, confronted him about his attitude. And her words changed his whole perspective. She said: "You know what? A day will come when Luke" their three-year-old son "will miss the mark, and fall short. He'll be brokenhearted, and will think his champion dad would never understand. But there will be this videotape, of a day in Sydney, where an example of how to lose with dignity was set. And I'll show it to him, and I'll tell him that I never loved his dad more."[26]

Now there's a wife who knows the importance of a good role model for her son. We all need models in our lives, don't we? Examples, heroes, people who will show us what is possible. We need people to inspire us and to give us hope. But think about this. Jesus is our perfect model. He shows us how a person filled with God's Spirit can live: Kind, forgiving, generous, caring and strong; being willing to sacrifice everything for his or her friends and even praying for their enemies.

Want to know what God looks like? Just take a look at Jesus. Without Him we might make some strange decisions about who God really is. Without Jesus we would have no hope of eternal life, either. He is not only our teacher, our model, and our example, but He is also our Savior.

Years ago a man named Bill McCartney left a successful coaching career in football to spend more time with his family and to work on his marriage. Eventually, he founded Promise Keepers, a Christian men's organization that encourages men to be better husbands and fathers. And Bill's wife was instrumental in making changes in their marriage, too.

After years of taking second place, she began insisting that Bill pencil her into his schedule every week. That worked for a while, but sometimes other things took priority over their date time. So one day, Bill's wife told him again to put her name on his calendar, but this time in ink, saying: "It's ink or nothing."[27] You know, that is a pretty good description of commitment. "It's ink or nothing."

Now, when God made a commitment to us, it was written in more than pencil. In fact it was written in more than ink. It was written in blood, the blood of our Lord Jesus Christ. Without Jesus we could believe all kinds of strange things about God. Without Jesus we would have no model for living a good and godly life. Without Jesus we would have no hope of eternal life with God. And finally, without Jesus we would not be able to reach out and touch God. This is our faith. If you want to know what God is like, just look at Jesus.

There is a story about a father who, on a dark, stormy night, in the midst of the thunder's crash and the lightning's flash, awakened and thought of his small son alone in his room upstairs, who might be afraid. So he rushed upstairs with his flashlight to check on the boy to see if everything was all right. He was flashing his light around in the room when the boy awakened, and said, "Who's there? Who's in my room?" The father's first thought was to flash the light in the face of the boy, but then he thought, "No, if I do that, I'll only frighten him more." So instead, he turned the light on his own face, and the little boy said, "Oh, it's you, Dad." And his father said, "Yes, it's me. I was just checking on things. Everything's okay, so go on back to sleep." And the little boy did.[28]

Like that father, God wanted to release us from our fears, fears about dying, fears of our own unworthiness. And so, he shined a light on His own face. We saw the face of Jesus and we knew it was the face of God. How do we touch God? Well, we begin with Jesus. *"Worthy is the Lamb."* Amen.

Looking For God's Footprints

Genesis 45:1-15

Then Joseph could no longer control himself before all those who stood by him, and he cried out, "Send everyone away from me." So no one stayed with him when Joseph made himself known to his brothers. And he wept so loudly that the Egyptians heard it, and the household of Pharaoh heard it. Joseph said to his brothers, "I am Joseph. Is my father still alive?" But his brothers could not answer him, so dismayed were they at his presence. Then Joseph said to his brothers, "Come closer to me." And they came closer. He said, "I am your brother, Joseph, whom you sold into Egypt. And now do not be distressed, or angry with yourselves, because you sold me here; for God sent me before you to preserve life. For the famine has been in the land these two years; and there are five more years in which there will be neither plowing nor harvest. God sent me before you to preserve for you a remnant on earth, and to keep alive for you many survivors. So it was not you who sent me here, but God; he has made me a father to Pharaoh, and lord of all his house and ruler over all the land of Egypt. Hurry and go up to my father and say to him, 'Thus says your son Joseph, God has made me lord of all Egypt; come down to me, do not delay. You shall settle in the land of Goshen, and you shall be near me, you and your children and your children's children, as well as your flocks, your herds, and all that you have. I will provide for you there--since there are five more years of famine to come--so that you and your household, and all that you have, will not come to poverty.' And now your eyes and the eyes of my brother Benjamin see that it is my own mouth that speaks to you. You must tell my father how greatly I am honored in Egypt, and all that you have seen. Hurry and bring my father down here." Then he fell upon his brother Benjamin's neck and wept, while Benjamin wept upon his neck. And he kissed all his brothers and wept upon them; and after that his brothers talked with him.

There was once a farmer who didn't believe in God and often made fun of people who did. And one day he wrote a letter to the editor of a local newspaper, saying: "I plowed on Sunday. I planted on Sunday. I cultivated on Sunday and I hauled in my crops on Sunday. And even though I never went to church on Sunday, I harvested more bushels per acre than all of those Christians who never missed a church service."[29]

When I heard that story, I just shuttered a little, because it reminded me so much of the story Jesus told about a farmer who kept building bigger barns for his crops, only to find that his life was going to end that night.[30] You know what? Going to church on Sunday is not what saves a person, but it is a measure of what is in a persons' heart. And most importantly, all of us including Christians will one day come face-to-face with our Maker and will have to give an account of what we did do with our Sundays.

Let us pray: May the words of my mouth and the meditations of each of our hearts be acceptable in Your sight, O God, our Rock and our Redeemer. Amen.

Like those faithful Christian farmers who watched their unbelieving neighbor bring in a huge crop, Joseph must have been perplexed by the fact that his God, the one who had spoken to him through dreams, would allow him to be sold into slavery and taken to a foreign land. I would imagine that he sometimes wondered where God was in it all.

Joseph, as a young boy, was loved more by his father than any of his brothers. And it was no secret. His father even went so far as to give Joseph a very special coat. And his brothers hated Joseph because of that. So they schemed to get rid of this dreamer brother of theirs. When their father wasn't around they stripped him of his special coat and threw Joseph into a deep dry well. They talked about killing him but as it happened, they sold him to traders instead. The brothers told their father that a wild animal must have killed Joseph because all they could find was his coat. Joseph's father was almost destroyed as he wept bitterly for his lost son.

Joseph was taken to Egypt where he knew no one and probably missed his family and his home very much. But even so, Joseph worked very hard for a man named Potiphar. He was such a good worker in fact that Potiphar put Joseph in charge of all the other servants. After a while Potiphar's wife, a selfish and manipulative person, had Joseph thrown into prison because he refused to yield to her wishes and "sin against God." Things looked bad for Joseph. But God helped him warn about a great drought that was coming. The king was so impressed with Joseph's insight and skills that he let Joseph out of prison and placed him second in command over Egypt. Joseph was put in charge of storing and serving all of Egypt's food. One day his brothers came to him because their family was starving. Without knowing that Joseph was their long lost brother, they bowed down to him and asked for help.

For a while it looked as though Joseph was thinking about getting even. But then a revelation from God broke through and his love for his brothers came flooding forth in a river of tears. You see, Joseph was an extraordinary man. He understood the character of God and was able to see the big picture. He was able to look back on his experiences, and see God's footprints, even, during the most difficult times in his life.

Now moving a little closer to our own history, we can see that John Wesley, the founder of Methodism, like Joseph also experienced God's footprints early on in his life. You've probably heard the story. Wesley's father, Samuel, was a dedicated pastor, but there were some in his parish who did not like him. On February 9, 1709, a fire broke out in the parsonage at Epworth, possibly set by one of Samuel's enemies. Young John, not yet six years old, was stranded on an upper floor of the building.

Two neighbors rescued him just seconds before the roof caved in. One neighbor stood on the other's shoulders and pulled young John through the window. Samuel Wesley said, "Come, let us kneel down. Let us give thanks to God. He has given me all my eight children. Let the house go. I am rich enough." Later in life, John referred to himself as a "brand plucked out of the fire,"[31] often giving thanks to God for His mercy.[32] From that day forward an ideal was planted in the life of John Wesley. Through his father's thankfulness, John was able to recognize God's presence through a fire that destroyed his family home and almost took his own life. Likewise, Joseph felt God's presence even when his brothers treated him cruelly. Both John and Joseph were able to look back on very difficult times in their lives, and amazingly see God's footprints there.

There are two parts to the process that all United Methodist pastors have to go through. There is an educational track and there is the church track. The church track was, for me, like "Looking for God's Footprints," because it was there that I was asked to look back over my life. And when I made a conscious effort to do that, amazingly I was able to see God's footprints all through my life. In a more recent time I recalled God's footprints, was during my mother's struggle with cancer. For several years I watched as my father showered her with tenderness, patience, gentleness and love. And I was convinced that this was an agape-like love that I knew could have only come from God. God was continuing to reveal Himself to me through the character of my father. I have always been amazed at how God blesses me even during difficult times.

Joseph had lots of time in Egypt to reflect on the fact that his brothers had sold him into slavery, and through that reflection he was able to finally reach the point where he could honestly say to his brothers: *God sent me to preserve life. God sent me before you to preserve for you a remnant. It was not you who sent me, but God.*[33] At that a revelation breaks in upon the entire family and a newness is created. A freshness is born that negates the past and brings salvation to God's people.

As a boy, Joseph had dreamed that he would be a ruler. But, now, as an adult, he is ruler-lord over a whole empire. Why? Well because he was in the will of God. Joseph was the conduit through which Israel's salvation would come. As Joseph was faithful to God, new life was given to Israel. In that sense, Joseph was a forerunner of Jesus Christ. And as God works through Jesus Christ, even today, a newness is created, a freshness also is born, a freshness that will change our past, redefine our present, and open up our future for God's glory.

Here's the point I want us to not miss in Joseph's story. He said to his brothers: *"Do not be afraid. Am I in the place of God? Even though you intended to do harm to me, God intended it for good."*[34] I think that this is the most amazing part of the story, because in Joseph's statement he reveals that he sees God working most powerfully during the very darkest time of his life. Joseph is able to look back on the time when he was sold into slavery and say: I know for a fact that God was with me. And maybe, maybe it was even God's own hand that delivered me into Egypt. Now, that is something to think about.

Maybe you have had a dark time in your life, similar to Joseph's. Perhaps you too, can recall something that was once very painful. Maybe you're going through a painful time right now. If so, remember the words of the prophet Jeremiah, as he spoke for the Lord, saying: *I know the plans I have for you, plans for your welfare and not for your harm, to give you a future with hope.*[35]

God's desire for us is to be able to take even the most painful of our experiences, even the darkest of our days, and work through them, so that God can bring: Good out of bad, wholeness out of brokenness, and ultimately, Life out of death. Out of an understanding like that will come, a future filled with hope as we take to heart God's promise, when He said: *I know the plans I have for you, plans for your welfare and not for your harm.* So just remember, even during the darkest time, even during a very painful situation, even when you are tempted to ask: "God where are You; where are You?" Remember that God is there and He is working on the plans He has for you.

You know, it seems a little cruel that God allowed Joseph to be taken into Egypt, but consider the alternative. His brothers were going to kill him. So really, if you think about it, it was out of the graciousness of God that a caravan of traders was sent to save him, and carry him to Egypt where he could hear God speaking to him, more clearly, and where God could work more powerfully through him to save all of Israel. We need to remember that God does have a plan for every situation, a plan not for harm but for good. Amen.

Excellent Living

<u>Romans 12:1-8</u>
I appeal to you therefore, brothers and sisters, by the mercies of God, to present your bodies as a living sacrifice, holy and acceptable to God, which is your spiritual worship. Do not be conformed to this world, but be transformed by the renewing of your minds, so that you may discern what is the will of God--what is good and acceptable and perfect. For by the grace given to me I say to everyone among you not to think of yourself more highly than you ought to think, but to think with sober judgment, each according to the measure of faith that God has assigned. For as in one body we have many members, and not all the members have the same function, so we, who are many, are one body in Christ, and individually we are members one of another. We have gifts that differ according to the grace given to us: prophecy, in proportion to faith; ministry, in ministering; the teacher, in teaching; the exhorter, in exhortation; the giver, in generosity; the leader, in diligence; the compassionate, in cheerfulness.

There was once a young man who believed that buying his first van would be the epitome of all his dreams. He worked hard and saved his money and finally the day arrived when he was able to purchase his van. It was beautiful, loaded, and luxurious. It was the result of perfect engineering and design. And the young man had every right to expect a great deal from this mechanical marvel as he drove it off the lot with pride. The next day, however, the van came back to the lot on a tow-truck. It was bent and battered, obviously un-drivable.

Shortly thereafter the young man stormed into the sales office, demanding not only a complete refund, but also threatening to sue for medical damages. "What happened?" asked the startled salesman. "Well," he said, "I bought your van, drove it out to the interstate to give it a test run, set the cruise control, went to the back to make a cup of coffee, and it ran off the road!"[36]

Now, I suspect that we all have a desire to put our lives on cruise control from time to time. And we almost hunger to just sit back, and enjoy the benefits of our modern world. And because we are constantly, in this technological world of ours, being promised the best of the best, many tend to hunger for excellence, as well. You know, there just seems to be a universal appreciation for excellence, so shouldn't we be seeking that same thing, in the way we live? Isn't there a philosophy of life that will help us find excellence not only in how we build our cars, but also in how we raise our children or grandchildren, treat our neighbors, and relate to ourselves and to God? Isn't there a plan somewhere that we can follow to help us find excellence in all areas of our lives?

Well, you may have already guessed that the answer is "yes," and it is found in these words written by the Apostle Paul. He said: *I appeal to you, brothers and sisters, by the mercies of God, to present your bodies as a living sacrifice, holy and acceptable to God, which is your spiritual worship and reasonable service.*[37] In this passage Paul brings to us, a picture of each of us standing before God, created in God's image, with dignity, excellence, and splendor, as nothing less than a living sacrifice. Not slain on an altar, but living. We are supposed to live fully and faithfully in harmonious relationship with ourselves, our neighbors, and with God.

Paul continues: *And do not be conformed to this world, but be transformed by the renewing of your minds, so that you may discern what is the will of God -- what is good and acceptable and perfect.*[38] There it is. That is what many are hungering for. We want what is excellent. But how do we obtain such excellence?

First, excellence requires discipline, similar to what Olympic contestants subject their lives to. But somehow we have convinced ourselves that it's okay to settle for less. One old preacher[39] objected to church members who were content saying: "Oh, I'm just an average Christian." Now, it may be true that we are not yet perfect or that we may even be just a little average in certain areas, but more, much more can be made of what God has given to us.

In the movie, Lawrence of Arabia, Lawrence is portrayed as a man torn between a lofty vision of unity, which would have required a sacrifice from him, and ordinary life. He longed for the comfort of the ordinary life and, he dreaded his vision with all of its, demands. But he decided to follow his vision anyway, and that's what made him so extraordinary.[40] You know, you can't expect to achieve excellence if your efforts are only half-hearted. No you have to be willing to go the extra mile.

For example, Leonardo Da Vinci worked for 10 years on his masterpiece: "The Last Supper." He was often so absorbed in his work that he forgot to eat for days at a time. And Luther Burbank, who was a genius with plants, at one time personally conducted over 6,000 experiments searching for a solution until a particular problem was solved and excellence was obtained. As it turns out, effort almost always results in excellence, and the same is true with the Christian life. Jesus told His disciples: *If anyone will come after Me, let them deny themselves, and take up their cross and follow Me.* Go that extra mile in your Christian life, Jesus says.

Now, I'm sure that there are people who come to worship just so they can say that have done their weekly duty and feel good about it. And I'm sure that there are others who slip out the back doors of a church, hoping that no one will notice them or ask them to do anything special. But, don't you know, can't you see, that there is no victory, no joy, and no excellence in living that way? People who do nothing for their faith most likely have a faith that does nothing for them. Excellence requires effort, and it begins with discipline.

It also requires direction. Someone once asked Winston Churchill why so many people of his own age had failed in business and professional life. And he responded: "Because they had no clear-cut goals." Plans and goals, set so as to achieve the excellent things in life are so very important in going forward in your walk with the Lord.

There once was an old story about a soldier. It went like this. There was a soldier whose job was to guard a prisoner with his life. But when the soldier was later called bring his prisoner forward, the prisoner was gone. And the soldier's excuse was: "Well, I was busy here and there, and the prisoner escaped." Sound familiar? That's the story of our lives. More often than not, we are busy "here and there." We forget to focus our lives, and so many important things somehow elude us.

Years ago there was a pole vaulter who showed a lot of promise. In practice he could perform with the best of his teammates. Unfortunately, though, whenever he competed in front of a crowd, he completely lost his ability. In order to overcome this problem, his coach had him put a picture of himself in his room where he was clearing the bar in perfect form. The coach wanted him to see his goal, and to see that he could do it. He wanted him to have a positive image to aspire to.

So, let me ask you this question. Do you have a positive picture of the kind of person you would like to be? How about substituting a picture of Christ for a picture of yourself? That would do it, wouldn't it? We already have the image of Jesus Christ as the kind of perfection we can aspire to. His life was excellence personified, and He is the direction towards which we must move. But having the image of Christ to aspire to and working hard to reach that goal is not enough. Each and every one of us must also have made an important decision answering the question: Am I in or am I out?

Jesus said to His disciples: *Whosoever will save their life shall lose it! And whosoever will lose their life for My sake shall find it. For what has a person profited, if they shall gain the whole world, and lose their own soul?* Are we for Christ, or are we against Him? Are we for Christ, or are we focused on centering our lives around, worldly things?

There was once a man named Count Zinzendorf who was traveling through Germany on his way to Paris: While there, he went into an art gallery to spend an hour or two admiring the works of some of the great masters. When he came to a picture of Christ on the cross, he stood transfixed before the scene as he read the words below the picture: "All this I did for thee. What hast thou done for me?" It was the turning point of the Count's life. He abandoned his plans to visit Paris, and returned home where he consecrated his life to the Lord. He devoted all that he was and all that he possessed to the master's service, and became the founder of a group of deeply devout Christians called the Moravians. And it was a group of Moravians who in turn witnessed to a young Anglican priest by the name of John Wesley.

Wesley's ship was being tossed by a terrible storm, and the quiet sure faith of these Moravian people greatly affected him. You see, Wesley knew these people had something he didn't have. They had an absolute trust concerning the divine intervention of God. When Wesley later attained that same assurance, he became a mighty spokesman for God and the founder of the Methodist faith.[41] And it all began with one man's decision to answer this question: "All this I did for thee. What hast thou done for me?"

Paul tells us that excellence is not found in being conformed, but by being transformed, transformed by the sanctifying work of God's Spirit that dwells within the believers' heart. We need discipline, and we need direction, yes we can't just go through life with it set on cruise control, and expect to rise above the crowd these days. But even before those things, we first need to make a decision, saying: Here am I, Lord God. All that I am and all that I have are Yours.

If you haven't already, I invite you today to make that decision. Just close your eyes, take a few moments to say: Here am I, Lord God, all that I am and all that I have are Yours.

Let us pray:
Oh God, we want to be a living sacrifice, holy and acceptable in Your sight. We want to give our lives completely and totally to You. But we are unable without Your divine intervention within our hearts.

Let your justifying and sanctifying Spirit enter into Your people today, and then walk with us (be with us) to bring us to that place of excellence that You so desire for us, as individuals, and as Your church. In Christ's name we ask these things. Amen.

The Eternal Value System

<u>Matthew 16:21-28</u>
From that time on, Jesus began to show his disciples that he must go to Jerusalem and undergo great suffering at the hands of the elders and chief priests and scribes, and be killed, and on the third day be raised. And Peter took him aside and began to rebuke him, saying, "God forbid it, Lord! This must never happen to you." But he turned and said to Peter, "Get behind me, Satan! You are a stumbling block to me; for you are setting your mind not on divine things but on human things." Then Jesus told his disciples, "If any want to become my followers, let them deny themselves and take up their cross and follow me. For those who want to save their life will lose it, and those who lose their life for my sake will find it. For what will it profit them if they gain the whole world but forfeit their life? Or what will they give in return for their life? "For the Son of Man is to come with his angels in the glory of his Father, and then he will repay everyone for what has been done. Truly I tell you, there are some standing here who will not taste death before they see the Son of Man coming in his kingdom."

A young woman, talking to a visiting evangelist said: "I don't dare give my life completely to the Lord for fear that He will send me to China as a missionary." The evangelist thought for a moment then asked: "But if on a cold, snowy morning a little bird came to you, half-frozen, pecking at your window. And if it would let you take it in and feed it, and put itself entirely in your power, what would you do? Would you take it in your hand and crush it? Or would you give it shelter, food, and care?"

And at that, a new light came into the woman's eyes and she said: "Oh, I see what you are saying. You're saying that I can trust God." Two years later she again met the evangelist and she told of how she had finally, abandoned her life to God. And then her face lit up with a smile and she said: "And do you know where God is going to let me serve? In China!"

Why do people inherently resist turning control of their lives over to God? Well, there are many reasons, I suppose, but what people say the most are things like: "I don't really trust that God will handle my life in the way I would want Him to handle it." Or, "I'm afraid of what God might ask me to do." Or, "I'm afraid of what I might have to give up." The nature of releasing control to God is, sometimes, difficult to do.

Let us pray: May the words of my mouth and the meditations of each of our hearts be acceptable in Your sight, O God, our Rock and our Redeemer. Amen.

I like the story of a young man who was eager to make it to the top. One day he went to a well-known millionaire and asked him the first reason for his success. And the businessman answered without hesitation, "Hard work." After a lengthy pause the young man asked: "Well, what is the second reason?" When Jesus speaks to His disciples about His destiny, to suffer, to die, and to be raised again, Simon Peter is sure that there must be an easier way.

When my children were young I decided to go back to school and my choices for Majors were Computer Science and Accounting, because, you see, I am just naturally a logical thinker. You may be too. Like many of us, Peter was a logical thinker, as well. And in response to Peter's logical thinking, Jesus said: *"Get behind me, Satan! You are a stumbling block to me; for you are setting your mind not on divine things but on human things."*

One of the early church fathers, a man named Origen, suggested that when Jesus said to Peter, *"Get behind me, Satan,"* what He actually meant was: "Peter, your place is behind Me not in front of Me. It's your job to follow Me in the way that I choose; it's not for you to try to lead Me in the way YOU would like Me to go."[42]

Now, certainly what Jesus said immediately after His rebuke of Peter would support that interpretation. He told all of them, including Peter: *"Deny yourself, and take up your cross, and follow Me."* In other words He was saying something like: Your job is to get on this new roller coaster ride with Me. There will be many dangerous twists and turns in the tracks, but I promise you it will never be dull. It will mean putting someone other than yourself first, being concerned not so much with what you want, but what God wants for you. It won't be easy and sometimes it won't be much fun, but it will never be boring."[43]

First, Jesus calls Peter *"Satan."* Second, Jesus says, *"Get behind me."* Third, Jesus tells Peter he is a *"stumbling block."* And finally, He tells him that *"his mind is set on human things, not divine."* Peter seems to think only of the easy road. And, though he does recognize Jesus, he still doesn't fully comprehend his call to release control to God.

Today's lesson teaches us to look beyond those things that we can visually see with our eyes and physically touch with our hands. It teaches us to go beyond this worldly value system, to go beyond our own common sense and to embrace the value system which is eternal. When Jesus walked this earth He lived a life that was directed by that eternal value system. He led a life of love and compassion. He mirrored His heavenly Father; He said: *"I do only what I see my Father in heaven do."* Jesus, though He was human like you and me looked past human logic to God's way of thinking. And that is what He teaches us to do, as well.

You know, Jesus was different then we are. He had a power that is not available to us. But the scriptures tell us that He chose to set that power aside when He came to earth and took on human form. He chose to become like us. Listen to this passage from Paul's letter to the Philippians. He writes: *Let the same mind be in you that was in Christ Jesus, who, though He was in the form of God, did not regard equality with God as something to be exploited, but emptied Himself taking the form of a slave, being born in human likeness. And being found in human form, He humbled Himself and became obedient to the point of death – even death on a cross.*[44] Yes, Jesus, who was and still is fully divine, became human for a brief time in history, so that He could open a pathway to God. And by opening that pathway to God He also showed us the way to our "true selves." He showed us that our true identity comes not from worldly thinking but from the One who created us. He showed us that our true identity comes from God. In other words Jesus tells us, in order for you to be your "truest" self you need to think the way God thinks.

But we have this common sense that tells us things like: In order to be happy: Our standard of living must be high, we need to have the perfect family without problems or flaws, we need to have not just a comfortable home, but one that is as least as good as the Smith's or the Jones' down the street. But, let me ask. Can true joy be found in things? Can we say that to live in this way would fill the deep longing that we all have for a meaningful and fulfilling life? I would say no to these questions. I would say no, because we were created for a bigger purpose. I would say no, because true contentment cannot to be found in the superficial things of this world. We are created in God's image. All human beings are created in God's image. God has a divine purpose for each one of us. And we were not created to live and manage a life that meets only the standards of this world. We are setting our goals, way too low. We are called to seek a better, a higher life, a life that is centered upon divine things. We are called to seek a life that this world cannot define for us.

Through this passage Jesus speaks to us, saying: "Seek the greater value. Do not stop with only what you can see and touch and feel. Seek the real value, the value that will last forever. Seek that which is possible through the yielding of your life to God. Set your mind on divine things, God's value system. Seek that which is centered upon God."

What do you think was going through Peter's mind, that day, when he said to Jesus: *"Lord, this must never happen to You"*? I've always thought that Peter didn't want to see Jesus suffer. But, this time as I was thinking about Peter's words, I began to wonder if there was more. Maybe Peter was thinking about the suffering that was in store for him if he did, indeed, follow Jesus. And, Jesus did respond a little later, saying: *"If any want to become my follower, you are going to have to deny yourself, and take up your cross and follow me."* He says: You will have to walk the road I am walking, Peter, and He says that that walk is not going to be easy.

Bob Hodges, a Presbyterian minister in Tennessee, tells about duck hunting with a friend of his. His friend, Riley, who had just recently given his life to Christ, began to ask some serious questions about his Christian walk. It seemed that Riley's old friends were making it very difficult for him to remain consistent in his obedience to Christ. They seemed to delight in trying to get him to fall back into the old patterns of life. And they ridiculed him for spending so much time with "the preacher." So Riley asked: "Why is it preacher, that I'm having more trouble since I became a Christian than I ever did when I was lost?" And the pastor answered with a question, saying: "When a couple of ducks fly over, and you shoot and kill one and injure the other. They both fall into the lake. But which one do you go after first?"

"Well," Riley said, "that's easy. I go after the injured one first. The dead one's not going anywhere!" And the preacher said: "Well, that's the way it is with the devil. He goes after the Christian, the one who is grasping for that life in Christ. He's not going to bother with the non-Christian, who is still dead in his sin. He's going after the one who has life. You see, the minute you give your life to Christ, you'd better get ready, 'cause the devil is going to come after you, and it's not going to be easy."[45]

If we are going to be followers of Christ, well, there are going to be crosses we will have to bear. Jesus said: "Deny your "selves" and take up your cross. In this statement, I believe that Jesus was addressing a "false self," a "false self" within us that has been defined by the world. Maybe what we are actually being called to do is to make a choice between our "false self," the self which the world trains us to be and our "true selves," the "self" which is created in God's image. One of the most dramatic shifts from the "false self" to the "true self" is the conversion of C. S. Lewis.

C. S. Lewis was an agnostic. He didn't believe that human beings had the ability to know that there was a God. But one day he was surprised by the God that he didn't think he could know about. And later, he wrote extensively about his relationship with the Lord, saying: "Christ says, give me everything. I don't want so much of your money and so much of your work – I want you. I have not come to torment your natural or your 'false' self, but to kill it. No half-measures are any good. I don't want to cut off a branch here and there. I want to have the whole tree down. I don't want to drill the tooth, or crown it, but to have it out. Hand over the whole natural self instead, and I will give you in its place my own self."[46]

Possibly our cross-bearing is the struggle that takes place between our well developed, "false self" and our "true self" that God has already placed within us. Perhaps we are being invited to see ourselves differently. Perhaps God is inviting us into an indescribable freedom through the indwelling Spirit of Christ. Perhaps He is inviting us to be what we truly are in His eyes.

God has given each of us a priceless gift. He has given us the ability to take ownership of a "New" value system, an eternal value system. God invites us to enter into a freedom that comes through letting go of our "false self" and embracing the self that He has already placed within us. God invites us to go beyond human logic. God invites us to seek that higher purpose for our lives. Jesus said: *"Those who lose their life for my sake will find it."*

I like the story of a little girl who, in the process of growing up, discovered that more than anything else she wanted to be able to mow the lawn. Each summer she was told that she was too young. But the day came, however, when her parents decided that at last she was old enough to do the task. She did it with surprising skill and great delight, and having finished admiring her work, she began to cast long, envious glances across the fence into the neighbor's backyard, which also needed cutting. The neighbor, seeing her interest, said: "Sally, would you like to cut my lawn, too?" And the little girl enthusiastically said, "Yes." "Well, let's see, how about $30.00?" said the neighbor. And the little girl became very sad and she turned away, shaking her head. "What's the matter?" asked the neighbor. "I only have $20.00," said the little girl.[47]

If we are ever going to truly live in the abundance of Christ, we are going to have to start thinking like that little girl. Cutting the grass, for her, was not a sacrifice at all, but it was the greatest privilege she could ever have. Losing our lives for Christ is not a sacrifice, but it is the greatest privilege we could ever have.

Jesus said: *"Satan comes only to steal and kill and destroy. But I come that you may have life, and have it abundantly."*[48] As we move into God's eternal value system, we will begin to realize that losing our life for Christ is not a sacrifice at all, but instead, that it is the greatest privilege ever given to us. And as we progress down the pathway of thinking that moves us from this earthly value system to the one that is eternal, as we do that, then God will guide us into an abundant life, into a life that is beyond our common sense and human imagining. Jesus says: Those who take hold of God's eternal value system, thus *"losing their life for my sake, will find it."* They will find Life. Amen.

Whose Side Will You Choose?

Matthew 16:21-25

From that time on, Jesus began to show his disciples that he must go to Jerusalem and undergo great suffering at the hands of the elders and chief priests and scribes, and be killed, and on the third day be raised. And Peter took him aside and began to rebuke him, saying, "God forbid it, Lord! This must never happen to you." But he turned and said to Peter, "Get behind me, Satan! You are a stumbling block to me; for you are setting your mind not on divine things but on human things." Then Jesus told his disciples, "If any want to become my followers, let them deny themselves and take up their cross and follow me. For those who want to save their life will lose it, and those who lose their life for my sake will find it.

On Monday, October 2, 2006, a 32-year-old milkman entered a humble one-room schoolhouse with the intent of killing as many students as possible. But one student, Marian Fisher, the oldest of the five Amish girls who were murdered that day, tried to buy time so that her schoolmates to escape. There were ten of them in all, all girls, five of whom survived. And those five may owe their lives to Marian whose unselfish inter-actions created enough time for her classmates to escape.[49]

This was an incredible display of courage by a young girl who was so wrapped up in her classmate's safety, that she was willing to lay her own life on the line for them. Maybe our Amish friends have something to teach us about the matter of a Christ-like love for others.

Let us pray: May the words of my mouth and the meditations of each of our hearts be acceptable in Your sight, O God, our Rock and our Redeemer. Amen.

Jesus and His disciples were at Caesarea Philippi. Their ministry to this point had been a stunning success. Crowds pressed in on them everywhere they went. People eagerly reached out to touch this young teacher from Nazareth. The disciples themselves were caught up in the excitement of it all when Jesus asked them: *"Who do you say I am?"* and Simon Peter answered enthusiastically: *"You are the Christ, the Son of the living God!"* It was one of the most dramatic moments in the disciples' pilgrimage with Jesus. Then, Jesus changed the subject. He began to tell them that the crowds would soon turn against Him; that He would be crucified and on the third day that He would be raised. The disciples didn't know what to make of all this. Peter took Him aside and began to rebuke Him. *"Never, Lord!"* he said. *"This shall never happen to You!"* And Jesus turned to Peter and said. Well, you know what he said: *Get behind Me, Satan! You are a stumbling block to Me; you do not have in mind the things of God, but the things of men.*

Have you ever called one of your best friends "Satan"? Well, maybe, in jest, possibly you have. But when Jesus called Peter, Satan, He wasn't being funny. This was a firm rebuke: *Get behind Me, Satan! He said. You are a stumbling block to Me; you do not have in mind the things of God, but the things of men.* Then Jesus said something else quite shocking. He said: *If anyone would come after Me, they must deny themselves and take up their cross and follow Me. For whoever wants to save their life will lose it, but whoever loses their life for Me will find it.* What did He mean? Does it have anything to do with a teen-aged girl offering her own life to save her friends? To say the least, it's a disturbing statement.

Maybe you will remember hearing an old joke about a little country church in North Carolina that was having a service when a guy in a blue devil's costume suddenly intruded. It seemed he was a student at Duke University, home of the Blue Devils. He was on his way to a pep rally, but by mistake he stumbled fully dressed in his devil's costume into this prayer meeting, setting off a near panic. The simple folk began exiting through doors and windows. One rather stout lady became wedged in a pew and began to scream in fear. The young Duke student in the blue devils costume, embarrassed over the trouble he was causing, rushed toward her to help her. And as she saw him advancing, she raised her hand and said: "Stop! Devil, don't come any closer. I want you to know that I have been a member of this church for 25 years, but I've been on your side all the time!"

Last Sunday we were each challenged with the question: Whose side are you on? Do you think that Jesus could say to any of us here: *Get behind Me, Satan! You are a stumbling block to Me; you do not have in mind the things of God, but the things of men?* You see, Satan doesn't just use bad people to do his work. In fact, he most often uses good people who are only nominally committed. That's when he is most effective. That's why Christ says in Revelation chapter 3: *I know your deeds, that you are neither cold nor hot. I wish you were either one or the other! So, because you are lukewarm neither hot nor cold I am about to spit you out of My mouth.*[50] Now, those are strong words, as strong as the words spoken to Simon Peter, that day.

And so it's a very important question: Which side are you on? Which side will you choose? There can't be any sitting on the fence. Either you're for Christ or you are against Him. Let me propose a brief test. You can grade yourself. Here's the first question on the test: Is your faith sacrificial? That is, is your faith costing you something?

There are many people today who are under the misconception that you can be a follower of Jesus without bearing a cross. We have become a rather apathetic people when it comes to our faith, haven't we? Many of us are much more interested in following the stock market, or following our favorite football team, or following the crowd, than we are in following Jesus. We want salvation without sacrifice, and so our Christianity is pale and weak, lukewarm as Jesus put it.

In one of history's more notable speeches, Prime Minister Winston Churchill of Great Britain challenged his countrymen to give "blood, sweat and tears" to oppose Nazi Germany. In his own way, he was challenging them to take up a cross of sacrifice. You know, no real progress is ever made in this world unless somebody makes a commitment to something bigger than him or herself. That is true of every important endeavor in life, and especially in our faith life. We cannot live out our faith in a world that is fast moving away from God unless we are willing to sacrifice, unless we are willing to put God's agenda first. Following Jesus is a joyful business, but it is also a serious business. Our goal is to bring the world to Christ. In fact that's our mission statement; it's printed on the top of your bulletin. Our mission statement is: "Bringing Others to Christ through our Actions, Words and Deeds." We can't do that, if our efforts are only half-hearted, and if our faith is only lukewarm. Jesus knew that.

There is a powerful scene in the movie *Schindler's List*. In the beginning of the story a Czech business man named Oskar Schindler builds a factory in occupied Poland using Jewish labor because, in those tragic days at the start of World War II, Jewish labor was cheap. As the war progresses, however, and he learns what is happening to the Jews under Adolph Hitler, Schindler's motivations switch from profit to sympathy. He uses his factory as a refuge for Jews to protect them from the Nazis. As a result of his efforts, more than 1,100 Jews were saved from death in the gas chambers.

Now, you would think that Oskar Schindler would have felt quite pleased with himself, but at the end of the war he stands in the midst of some of the Jews he has saved, breaks down in tears, takes off his gold ring and says: "My God, I could have bought back two more people with this ring. These shoes? One more person. My coat? Two more people. This car? Ten more people." There he stands, not gloating but weeping with regret that he had not done more. I wonder if one day you and I as followers of Christ will ask ourselves: "Could I have done more? Have I truly borne the cross of Christ?" That is the first question on today's test: Is your faith sacrificial? Is it costing you something?

Here's the second: Do you spend most of your efforts looking out for yourself? Many people do, you know. In fact, that's what our society tells us to do. Whitney Houston, in a song that was hugely popular a few years back, particularly with many school choirs, told us that to love one's self is "the greatest love of all." Of course, Americans have a long history of fascination with self. Maybe some of you had to read a poem in school by Walt Whitman, titled, "Song of Myself." It begins: "I celebrate myself, and sing myself. I breathe the fragrance myself and know it and like it." Then, towards the end, Whitman writes: "Nothing, not God, is greater to one than ones' self is. Nor do I understand who there can be more wonderful than myself." Or if you don't remember that poem maybe you remember an old L'oreal commercial that summed it up this way, saying: "I'm worth it!" And we continue to be bombarded with commercials and ideologies that try and teach that we and not a Higher Power is at the very center of our existence.

It's no wonder that a recent study of one million senior high students revealed that, on leadership ability, 70 per cent thought they were above average, and only 2 per cent below. In the category "ability to get along with others," none of the students rated themselves below average, 60 per cent rated themselves as being in the top 10 per cent and twenty-five thought they were in the top 1 per cent when it came to getting along with others.

And just in case you think it's confined to teenagers, another survey found that 94 per cent of the teachers thought they were better than their average colleague. "Oh, how do I love myself? Let me count the ways."[51]

Sure, there is something to be said about a positive self-esteem. We do need to have a healthy sense of self respect in order to make a difference in the world, but at the same time, we were not put on this earth to look only after number one. Yes, as human beings created in the image of God, we are important. But we are no more important than every other man, woman, young person and child on this planet. Jesus said: *If anyone would come after Me, they must deny themselves and take up their cross and follow Me.* Do you live a sacrificial life? Does your commitment to serving God come first? Do God's purposes come first in what you decide to do on a day to day basis, or do you spend most of your efforts looking out for number one?

Here is the final question on the test: Do you trust God and God alone for your salvation? It would be easy to conclude from today's lesson that this is the whole story of our faith. Deny yourself, live sacrificially, take up your cross. But this is not the whole story. If it were so, Simon Peter would have been doomed, and so would we. Christ does not expect us to live under a heavy weight of guilt like Oskar Schindler, always feeling that we could have done more. No, instead we need a healthy balance of humility and self worth. A burden like the one Schindler carried would ultimately weigh us down and defeat us. And it was never God's intention that we would think of ourselves with self-disgust, like worms of the dust, of no value at all, hopeless "sinners in the hands of an angry God" as one 18th century pastor preached it. But instead God's message to us is that, we are of ultimate worth. Christ gave His life for us. This is where positive self-esteem comes from. It comes from knowing that even though we are not yet perfect, we are loved. We are loved by the Creator God who sent His son to die for us.

There is a story of a young boy from the slums of London named James, whose only refuge from the unpleasantness of poverty was the Roman Catholic school he attended. Somehow his mother had managed to enroll him in this parochial school that was located in a middle class neighborhood. In spite of the fact that he came from a poor family, James managed to fit in fairly well, in part because everyone wore the same uniform. But the uniform could not completely conceal years of malnutrition. James was small for his age and his skin still had the pallor that comes from a deficient diet. One day a physician came to the school to give medical examinations for all of the students. As James left the examination room, one of the nuns asked him what the doctor had to say about him. James answered: "He took one look at me and said, 'What a miserable specimen you are!'" The sister could see the hurt in James' eyes, but after a short pause his eyes brightened again and he said: "But he didn't know that I've had my first Communion, did he, Sister?"[52]

Wow, now that's what makes us special isn't it? Knowing that we are loved by Christ is why we can hold our heads high and say: God put me here for a reason, I am valuable in His sight, and He has a very unique and wonderful plan for my life. He loves me so much that He was willing to lay down His life for me, offering forgiveness and ultimately eternal life.

Now, I suspect that it is true that we are not all we should be. Some of us may be a little too self-involved. We confess we do not live as sacrificially as we should. But God loves us anyway with an unconditional love. Christ died for us. And because of that we can trust Christ and Christ alone for our salvation. So, whose side will you choose? I hope it will be God's side, for it is God who loves you when the world turns away. Are you ready to heed Jesus' call on your life? Have you made your choice?

My challenge to you today is to take the exam often asking: Is my faith sacrificial? Is it my desire to do "all the good I can" as far as I am able? And finally: Am I trusting in the work done on the cross of Christ, alone, for my salvation? Those are the questions before you.

Is my faith sacrificial? Is it my desire to do good all the time? Am, I trusting in Christ alone for my salvation? And if your answers are yes, then ask yourself: How, will my faith in God be a part of my life this week? Let each of us now individually, take a few moments with God, honestly talking with Him, about how well you scored on the exam. Am I living sacrificially; am I doing good to the best of my ability; and do I trust wholly in Christ for my salvation?

Oh, God, hear our prayers, transform us with Your justifying and sanctifying Spirit, and then send us out into the world to be faithful servants for You. In Christ's name we pray. Amen.

Straight Talk

Matthew 18:15-20
"If another member of the church sins against you, go and point out the fault when the two of you are alone. If the member listens to you, you have regained that one. But if you are not listened to, take one or two others along with you, so that every word may be confirmed by the evidence of two or three witnesses. If the member refuses to listen to them, tell it to the church; and if the offender refuses to listen even to the church, let such a one be to you as a Gentile and a tax collector. Truly I tell you, whatever you bind on earth will be bound in heaven, and whatever you loose on earth will be loosed in heaven. Again, truly I tell you, if two of you agree on earth about anything you ask, it will be done for you by my Father in heaven. For where two or three are gathered in my name, I am there among them."

There were two brothers who lived on adjoining farms. And one day they had a conflict. It was the first serious fight in their 40 years of working together. It began with a small misunderstanding, and grew into a major difference, and finally exploded into bitter words and was followed by weeks of silence. One morning, there was a knock on the older brother's door. He opened it to find a man with a carpenter's toolbox. "I'm looking for a few days' work," he said. "Perhaps you would have a few small jobs here and there that I could help with?" "Yes," said the older brother. "I do have a job for you. Look across the creek at that farm. That's my younger brother's house. Last week, there was a meadow between us, but then he took his bulldozer and dug a river between us. Well I'll show him. See that pile of old lumber? I want you to build an 8-foot fence between us. Then I won't have to see his place or his face anymore." The carpenter said: "Show me the nails and I'll do a good job."

Then the older brother had to go to town, so he left for the day. At sunset, when he returned, he couldn't believe what he saw. There was no fence there at all. The carpenter had built a bridge that stretched from one side of the river to the other, with handrails and all. And his younger brother was coming toward them, waving his arms and saying: "You're quite a guy; after all I've said and done to you." And amazingly, when the two of them met they embraced each other in brotherly love. Then they turned to see the carpenter leaving. "No, wait," said the older brother, stay a few days. I've a lot of other projects for you." "I'd love to," said the carpenter, "but I have other bridges to build."[53] As you all know, there is another carpenter, the Master Carpenter, the One from Nazareth who is also in the business of building bridges between brothers and sisters when they, too, fall into conflict.

Let us pray: May the words of my mouth and the meditations of each of our hearts be acceptable in Your sight, O God, our Rock and our Redeemer. Amen.

Jesus was divinely incarnate, but that doesn't mean that He was divinely naive. He knew that there were going to be disagreements and fights among well-meaning people who would later get together in His name. So, before He left, He set up a way for us to deal with disputes within God's church.

Now, when it comes to development, a church and a marriage are a lot alike. In a marriage, experts say that there are four stages of development: The honeymoon, the shock of reality, the adjustment and finally, the stage of quiet contentment. The fact is, for a marriage to be successful it must finally arrive and the fourth stage, that of contentment. But along that journey, in a church, just as in a marriage, there will be disagreements. That's not the issue, says Jesus. The issue is: How you will fight.

Jesus, very simply, lays down some ground rules for fighting fair. First of all, He recommends straight talk. If you've got a problem with someone or something in the church, deal with it directly, Jesus says. Instead of embarrassing that person in front of others, deal with it one-on-one if you can. And don't beat around the bush, either. Get right to the point. What Jesus says is this: "If your brother does wrong or your sister makes a mistake or you have a problem, speak to them for heaven's sake." Don't keep your mouth shut allowing it to churn inside of you and don't go and tell someone else about it either. According to Jesus, that's not a very good way to handle our discontent with others.

Once a school board member shared a concern with an older board member and the older and wiser board member said: "Share it with the board." "Oh, I don't know," said the younger man. "I'm fairly new. I don't know if I should do that or not." And at that, the now retired president of a large management firm looked his younger counterpart in the eye and said: "Son, there were times in my life when I could have spoken up and didn't and now I regret it. State your piece." So the timid, young man did that and to his surprise, it resulted in a significant change in school policy, a change that should have happened much earlier.[54]

But sometimes, it's difficult to decide to speak directly to another person, isn't it? And so we don't, or we do it behind the scenes in destructive ways, or we store it up inside and dump it out on some other poor soul, or group of people. Bosses often do that to employees and spouses often do that to each other. And church members are no different.

Straight talk; that is what Jesus prescribes. In a way that's what preachers and teachers do week after week. And sometimes whether you realize it or not it's uncomfortable for us to do, but we have a responsibility before God. You see, to not engage in "straight talk" from the pulpit or from the teacher's podium, is to discredit God's Word.

And for Christians, in general, to not engage in "straight talk" with one another is to do the same thing. When you have a complaint, talk first to the offending party, Jesus says. And the apostle Paul adds: *"Do it in a loving way."* And if that doesn't work, then get others involved. Jesus says: "Try to settle it with two or three others present." And if that doesn't work, well, then *"tell it to the church."* Here, I think, Jesus means a small group of responsible and discerning fellow believers. And finally, if the offender refuses to listen even to the church, then Jesus says: *"Let such a one be to you as a Gentile and a tax collector."* Wow! Now there's the passage we've all been waiting to get to. That's the tough one.

Okay, what did Jesus really mean here? Well, first of all, how did Jesus treat Gentiles and tax collectors? He treated them with patience and compassion. He treated them as someone outside the faith community, yes, but He also had concern for them. Jesus always received those who were outside the faith community. He even had table fellowship with them, which in His time, was something a person only did with someone they truly cared about.

And think about this. Isn't it interesting that Jesus was involved with Gentiles His whole life? Isn't it interesting that: The first to show up at His home were the Magi; the first to show up when Jesus was only a child, were Gentiles? And according to Matthew, the first person Jesus healed was the servant of a Gentile Centurion. And one day Jesus called a man named Matthew to be His disciple, who was a tax collector.

Jesus says: *"Love your neighbor as yourself and also love your enemy."* And so, even when we do have to treat a brother or sister in the Lord as if they are outside the church, we must continue to work with them in gentle and loving ways. Why, well so that God might be able to use our efforts to bring that person back into the worshipping community. That's the whole idea.

Jesus tells us that we should deal with problems in the church, first with straight talk, then due process, but most of all, with grace, the same grace that Jesus showed to Gentiles and tax collectors. Jesus also said: *I tell you, if two of you agree on earth about anything you ask, it will be done for you by my Father in heaven.*[55]

You know what, there is much power when Christians work together, pray together, and discern God's will together. There is much power, Jesus says, in the church when members are united and reconciled, and in agreement with one another. And, when that happens Jesus says: *"There I am in the midst of them."* That is the crowning conclusion of our passage for today. The strength of the Christian community is dependent upon healthy "relationships," between us, one to another, because when we are reconciled one to another, then it just naturally follows that we are reconciled to God, Christ is there among us. And don't forget this. Jesus knows our hearts, He knows if we are reconciled to our brother or our sister, and ultimately if we are reconciled to God. So, if you have a complaint with someone. Take Jesus' advice, take that first step, go and talk with that person privately. Gather in the name of Christ, just the two of you, where the Carpenter from Nazareth will build a healing bridge of reconciliation between your hearts. He is the Master builder of bridges. He is the Master healer of relationships, as well. He built a bridge between God and humanity and, when necessary, He can also build a bridge between you and your brother or sister in Christ.

Let us pray:
O Lord God, we ask that You heal Your church, today. Break down the fences that divide, remove the fences that we have built in anger or despair. Take away the hurt and the pain that paralyzes us and keeps us from experiencing Your peace and Your joy and Your love. Take away those things that keep us from functioning as Your church in this world.

Help us to forgive. Help us to repent. Help us to experience reconciliation within the Body of Christ. Heal us we pray and then send us out in Your name to help others find that Ultimate Reconciliation, as well. These things we ask in the precious and holy name of Jesus Christ, our Lord and Savior. Amen.

Unmerited Favor

<u>Matthew 20:1-16</u>
"For the kingdom of heaven is like a landowner who went out early in the morning to hire laborers for his vineyard. After agreeing with the laborers for the usual daily wage, he sent them into his vineyard. When he went out about nine o'clock, he saw others standing idle in the marketplace; and he said to them, 'You also go into the vineyard, and I will pay you whatever is right.' So they went. When he went out again about noon and about three o'clock, he did the same. And about five o'clock he went out and found others standing around; and he said to them, 'Why are you standing here idle all day?' They said to him, 'Because no one has hired us.' He said to them, 'You also go into the vineyard.' When evening came, the owner of the vineyard said to his manager, 'Call the laborers and give them their pay, beginning with the last and then going to the first.' When those hired about five o'clock came, each of them received the usual daily wage. Now when the first came, they thought they would receive more; but each of them also received the usual daily wage. And when they received it, they grumbled against the landowner, saying, 'These last worked only one hour, and you have made them equal to us who have borne the burden of the day and the scorching heat.' But he replied to one of them, 'Friend, I am doing you no wrong; did you not agree with me for the usual daily wage? Take what belongs to you and go; I choose to give to this last the same as I give to you. Am I not allowed to do what I choose with what belongs to me? Or are you envious because I am generous?' So the last will be first, and the first will be last."

One day a rich young ruler came enthusiastically running up to Jesus and asked: "What must I do to be saved?" And Jesus answered: "Keep the law." "This I have done from my youth up," the young man said. And then Jesus replied: "Then there is one thing that you lack. Go and sell all that you have and give it to the poor. Then come, follow me." We are told that the young man walked away sad, for he had great wealth. And Jesus concluded: It will be hard for a rich man to enter the Kingdom of God.

The disciples had been watching the dynamics of this happening and they were quite disturbed. Jewish tradition had always taught that God had especially blessed a rich person and that is why they were rich. In their way of thinking, if a wealthy person could not receive salvation, then how could a poor person have any hope? So they asked: Who then can be saved? And finally, Peter drew the question even more clearly into focus, saying: "Lord, we have given up everything, riches and all, to follow you." What about us, Lord? What about us? And in response Jesus told a story. It went like this. During the harvest time of the year, at 7 in the morning a wealthy landowner went to the Town Square to hire laborers to work in his vineyard. He began hiring early in the day and continued hiring even until the last hour. Now, he had made an agreement with each worker individually. He agreed to pay each of them one denarius for the day's work. However, in the evening when it came time to get paid, those who worked only one hour got paid as much as those who had worked all day. The ones who had worked longer cried out: Hey, we worked all day and these other people have only worked for one hour. Why should they get as much money as us? Humanly speaking, the people had a legitimate complaint. But listen to the landowner answer. He said that each person had agreed to work for one denarius and true to his word, he had paid each of them one denarius. There are several things we can draw from this parable. First, everyone is important to God. Jesus said that all the workers deserved a full day's pay. In this parable we learn that the person who comes late is just as important to God, as the one who comes early.

A writer named Jens Peter Jacobsen, tells about a man who rejected God. As he grew older, he secretly desired the peace of faith, but he refused to come humbly to God, even during the last days of his life. It seems that fate had been harsh to him with death visiting those whom he loved most. Tenaciously, he held on to disbelief, even though he wanted the peace of God. In the last hour of his life, he refused to see the pastor, though secretly he wanted forgiveness and consolation. His physician, who loved him, was moved by what he observed and whispered: "If I were God, I would save the man who repents, at the last minute."[56]

People are equally important to God. And I believe that there is a special tug on God's heart when one person refuses to repent and turn to Him for salvation. We see evidence of this anguish in God's heart when Jesus weeps over the unrepentant city of Jerusalem. Yes, God longs for every person to be saved. But the problem with God saving those who blatantly refuse to love Him, is that, in order to do that, He would have to make a choice for that person. And God doesn't force anyone to love Him. We have to make the decision to love Him, on our own. Even so, those who do not love God are just as important to Him as those who do.

In certain ways, the love of our heavenly Father can be compared to the love of an earthly father. In Frederick Borsch's book, he writes: When my wife was expecting our first child, I found that I had an inordinate desire to have a son. I feel apologetic about that now. It seems rather sexist. But I had two sisters and no brothers as I was growing up, and I had always wanted to have a little brother. So, when Benjamin was born all my heart, more love than I knew I had, went out to him. But two years later when my wife was expecting again, I discovered that I had a very worrisome problem. How could I hide from our second child the fact that I could never love him or her as much as Benjamin? I must have thought that love was like a pie, I guess. The more people that came to share it, the smaller the slices had to be.

Then, as though to make matters worse, we had twins. But you can probably guess, what happened next. It was like a miracle to me. Suddenly I loved Matthew and Stuart with the same love with which I loved Benjamin, without taking any away from our first son. This was a strange new arithmetic, for me. The pie seemed to have become miraculously larger.[57]

God loves each and every person equally. His love can be compared to a huge ever-expanding pie. With each new person the pie grows to add in one more slice that is the same size as the first, not smaller, not larger, but equal. The first thing we learn from this parable is that all people are equally important to God. And the second thing we learn is that working in God's vineyard is rewarding. Jesus said: *About five o'clock the landowner went out and found others standing around; and he said to them, "Why are you standing here idle all day?" And they said to him, "Because no one has hired us." And the landowner said to them, "You also go into the vineyard."*[58] In other words, it is a privilege to work in God's vineyard. If there is any special payoff for coming early to labor in the Lord's field, it is the inner satisfaction that we receive from serving God in this world. And the key to understanding this second bit of wisdom is in remembering that the vineyard is the symbol of God's kingdom. The vineyard is God's new community, His new reality. The vineyard is the Church and God is the owner. The landowner owns the vineyard, lock, stock, and barrel. And we are privileged to labor in God's vineyard, where we receive the security that there will be adequate compensation for all. But the real pay is not the wage offered at the end of the day. The work itself is our gift, our immeasurable privilege. The work itself carries its own reward.[59]

First we learn that everyone is equally special to God. The second thing we learn is that there is great reward in this life for those who come early to labor in God's vineyard. And the third thing we learn is that we cannot fully comprehend the nature of God's grace toward us.

The grace of God, the unmerited favor of God is something that just humanly doesn't make sense to us. One pastor put it this way. He said: This parable goes against the business mentality that dominates our lives. We have always been taught: You get out of something directly in proportion to that which you put in. Yet, that is not what happened in Jesus' story. In our way of thinking, the laborers who came to the field late got something for nothing and the early laborers worked too hard for what they received.[60] But in God's reality the earlier workers received, not only, the daily wages, but also, the immeasurable privilege and inner satisfaction of the work itself.

You see, serving God is something other than a business transaction. Yet, because we live in a world of tenure and seniority, this story about laborers who work unequal hours and get equal pay, well, it just goes against our usual way of thinking. But, in this story we learn that God's grace is not based upon tenure or seniority or fairness, but rather upon His unmerited favor towards humanity.

Again and again in parables, sermons, and actions Jesus startles us. Things are not like they are supposed to be. The stories don't end as we expect them to. The good guys turn out to be the bad guys as the ones expected to receive a reward get chastised. The least are the greatest. The immoral receive forgiveness. Adults become like children. The religious, miss the heavenly banquet. The kingdom surprises us again and again by turning our world upside down. And indeed, this story, well, it goes against our usual ways of thinking. And I would imagine, for a "rich man," that one Jesus referred to earlier, that it would be, for him, much more difficult to accept.

Philip Yancey, a writer of Christian books, asserts that there is an "atrocious mathematics" at the heart of the gospel. He writes: Jesus' story makes no economic sense. But, that was His intent. He was giving us a parable about grace, which cannot be calculated like a day's wages. Grace is not about finishing last or first. It's not about arithmetic at all.[61]

After serving as a missionary for forty years in Africa, Henry C. Morrison became sick and had to return to America. As the ocean liner docked in the New York Harbor there was a great crowd gathered to welcome home another passenger on that boat. Morrison watched as President Teddy Roosevelt received a grand welcome home party after his African Safari. Resentment seized Henry Morrsion and he turned to God in anger saying: "That's not fair. I have come home after all this time and service to the church and there is no one, not even one person here to welcome me home."[62] How often does a loving mother hear her child complain: "That's not fair!" And sometimes, from a strictly objective standpoint, the child is right, what they are complaining about is not fair. But fairness is not a loving mothers' objective. Raising healthy, responsible children is her objective. So it is with God.

The scriptures teach us that our God is a righteous God (Old Testament), but they also teach us that justice is not God's primary concern (New Testament). God is not interested in balancing our virtues and our vices and then handing out rewards and punishments accordingly. God is interested in fashioning souls who can live with Him for all eternity. That is what the cross is all about. The old system of offering sacrifices for sin, even sins we may not be aware of, to an angry and wrathful God is done away with forever. Christ has borne all our sins upon the tree. That is why His passion and death was so horrific. He who knew no sin bore the sins of every person who has ever lived, your sin and my sin, on the cross of Calvary. And that's not fair. We ought to have to pay our own way. But instead, Jesus paid it for us.

And God's plan of grace is not fair for another reason. It's unequal. Murderers, thieves and adulterers receive the same forgiveness as Sunday school teachers and martyrs. There it is. It's not fair, but it's all done. The slate is wiped clean. Never again will anyone ever have to avoid God because of his or her unworthiness. And never again will anyone deserve to feel superior to anyone else. We may not be equals in the office or the business world or on the athletic field, but at the foot of the cross we are all sinners saved by grace.

There was once a man who died and went to heaven. And, of course, St. Peter met him at the Pearly Gates. St. Peter said: "Here's how it works. You need 100 points to make it into heaven. You tell me all the good things you've done, and I will give you a certain number of points for each item, depending on how good it was. When you reach 100 points, you get in." "Okay," the man says. "I was married to the same woman for 50 years and never cheated on her, not even in my heart." "That's wonderful," says St. Peter. "That's worth three points." "Three points" asks the man? Then he says: "Well, okay, I attended church all my life and supported its ministry with my tithes and my service." "Terrific!" say's St. Peter. "That's certainly worth a point." "One point? Well I started a soup kitchen in my city and worked in a shelter for homeless veterans." "Fantastic, that's good for two more points." "Two points!" The man cries. "At this rate the only way to get into heaven is by the grace of God!" St. Peter smiled. "There's your 100 points! Come on in!"[63] You know, we can try to rely upon our own righteousness to get into heaven, but it will never be enough. We cannot depend on our virtue, even if it's genuine. We can't even rely upon God's justice, for that matter. God is a righteous God, yes, but justice is not His primary concern. His primary concern is unmerited favor and generosity, for all people.

We get a little taste of that generosity as we take God up on the offer to be workers in His vineyard. But we will never fully understand in this lifetime, God's unmerited favor toward us.

Our God is a very generous God. And because of His unmerited favor, because of His generosity, you are perfect in God's eyes right now, not in your own right, but because of what Christ has already done on your behalf. If you haven't come to Christ before, come to Him now. Or, if you are holding back a certain area of your life, bring it to Him now. Lay it at the foot of the Cross. Do it now. Come to Him now, imperfection and all because God, in all of His generosity, is waiting for you with open arms. Amen.

Why?

Luke 13:1-9
At that very time there were some present who told him about the Galileans whose blood Pilate had mingled with their sacrifices. He asked them, "Do you think that because these Galileans suffered in this way they were worse sinners than all other Galileans? No, I tell you; but unless you repent, you will all perish as they did. Or those eighteen who were killed when the tower of Siloam fell on them-- do you think that they were worse offenders than all the others living in Jerusalem? No, I tell you; but unless you repent, you will all perish just as they did." Then he told this parable: "A man had a fig tree planted in his vineyard; and he came looking for fruit on it and found none. So he said to the gardener, 'See here! For three years I have come looking for fruit on this fig tree, and still I find none. Cut it down! Why should it be wasting the soil?' He replied, 'Sir, let it alone for one more year, until I dig around it and put manure on it. If it bears fruit next year, well and good; but if not, you can cut it down.'"

Once in a lifetime something happens on the world stage. Something happens that shapes the course of human events. And it seems we have lived more than a lifetime in only seven years: September 11, 2001 and the Tsunami and recent Hurricanes, have given us more than any one generation should have to endure.

Seven years ago this month a rock was dropped into the pond of this world, and the resulting ripples are still with us. Consider for a moment what was set in motion by the terrorist activities in 2001: Our nation's capital was attacked. Over 3000 people lost their lives. The Manhattan skyline was changed forever. The financial trade center for 150 nations was completely destroyed. The world's economy was greatly tested. And a long-standing almost invisible war is being fought, and will be fought, for years to come around the world. Now consider for a moment what has been set in motion from recent hurricanes: Unknown 1000's have lost their lives. Thousands of square miles of the United States has been destroyed. Over a hundred thousand homes have been destroyed. Millions of US citizens have been displaced. Eighty percent of one city, New Orleans was under water, as it actually became a part of the ocean. And thousands of children are now attending schools in other states.[64] That's the big picture and it says nothing of the tens of thousands of people here and abroad whose lives have been changed in ways that we may never know. Try to calculate the human toll emotionally and spiritually and you cannot. Only God can weigh such matters.

Let us pray: May the words of my mouth and the meditations of each of our hearts be acceptable in Your sight, O God, our Rock and our Redeemer. Amen.

We try in feeble ways to understand events like 911 and major hurricanes and Tsunamis. And in doing so, questions arise. Why is there so much evil in the world? Why does nature overwhelm us and destroy lives? Why do innocent people suffer? We ask questions like: Where was God on September 11? Where was God when 280,000 perished in the Tsunami? Where was God during destructive hurricanes? Why does He allow such awful things to happen? These are universal questions. They are as old as Job, and are asked by the wisest people among us. For years, humankind has sought after answers for such questions. And we are still searching.

We, as human beings, ask why, why, why? And this phenomenon of question asking is especially apparent in the Bible. If you were to look closely at the Bible you would find that one book has a disproportionate number of questions, the book of Job. Job has over 330 questions in its 42 chapters. Genesis, the first book of the Bible only has 160. And in the New Testament, Matthew has around 180. And that's odd because it seems that Jesus was asking questions all the time. Even in the book of Psalms with its 150 chapters there are only 160 questions. So why does the book of Job have so many more questions? Well, it's simple. It is because the book of Job deals with a horrible tragedy.

I'm sure you remember that Job was a righteous man. He was in right standing with God. He was God's servant and was loved by his Lord. Yet, God permitted "Satan" to test him. Consider what Job suffered. In one day he lost all of his possessions: seven thousand sheep, three thousand camels, five hundred yoke of oxen and five hundred donkeys. But it didn't stop there. He also lost a large number of his servants. And by sundown, Job had lost all of his children. In many ways current events, seem to echo the story of Job. A very large number of Americans have had their lives majorly changed by 911, Tsunamis and recent hurricanes. We have been hit, and hit hard. Now what?

Well first, we do what Job did when he learned of his loss. We allow ourselves to mourn. He was silent when he received the first two reports about his business and his livestock. Those could be replaced. But when he received the news that his children were lost, he fell to his knees and wept bitterly. Everything that had meaning in his life was gone. As he came into this world so Job felt he was leaving it, naked, without anything. And you wouldn't think it could happen, but it even got worse as Job's friends, the ones who should have been comforting him and mourning with him, accused him of having some hidden sin in his life.

Job's friends believed that when a great tragedy happened that it somehow had something to do with the unrighteousness of that person. And so, the question arose, was Job to blame for his own suffering? Well, no. At the very beginning God calls Job "blameless and upright." Yet, he still is not shielded from tragedy, a tragedy that has no rhyme or reason, a tragedy that was not caused by God, but happened anyway.

And over the past decade in some circles, the question has arisen again: Does God cause mighty winds to collapse 1,000's of homes in Mississippi, Alabama, and Louisiana and now Texas? Well, no. Did God have some purpose in all this? No. Were the people of those four states any more sinners than we are? No. Thank goodness, in our day and time, most of us know that there are other explanations for why we have disastrous storms, such as the one we've just seen. And Jesus, I think, would agree. Listen once again to our scripture reading for today.

Luke writes: *At that very time there were some present who told Jesus about the Galileans whose blood Pilate had mingled with their sacrifices. He asked them, "Do you think that because these Galileans suffered in this way they were worse sinners than all other Galileans?" "No, I tell you," Jesus said.*[65] In this text we have a tragic event in the life of Israel. It was headline news, everyone knew about it. You see, Israel had been conquered by Rome. And Rome's presence was a constant reminder that they were a nation under siege. The people learned to live with it but there remained a great tension, a religious underground had actually emerged to fight for freedom, because Pilate was such a ruthless ruler. It seemed that he decided to make an example of a group of Galilean Jews. He ordered his soldiers to go into the temple in the middle of the day, while tens of thousands of people were worshipping there, and execute them. This was done to send a message to the Jews: If you do not keep your region under control you will suffer the consequences of Rome's might.

Pilate sent a political and religious message by slaying a group of innocent people. Now the Galilean territory may have done something that set Pilate off but those in the Temple that day, quite likely, had nothing to do with it. They were, convenient. They were in the wrong place at an unfortunate time. Even so, some were still asking Jesus if these people died because they had sinned. Was this God's judgment because of their immoral living, they asked? And Jesus gives a very straight-forward answer. No, he says, it could have happened to anyone. And then the people continued with their questioning. They asked Jesus: *Those eighteen who were killed when the tower of Siloam fell on them -- do you think that they were worse offenders than all the others living in Jerusalem? No, Jesus said, but unless you repent, you will all perish just as they did.*[66]

Probably one of the most often asked questions during a time of tragedy is: Where is God? And the second most asked question could very well be: "Did God, out of His wrath, cause this?" And once again in our own day, we've heard those same questions. Where was God and does He cause things like 911 or Hurricanes? Well, I think this answers it best: Just as God was not in the cockpit of those four planes on 911 2001, He is not in hurricanes that rip through the Gulf Coast. God was not in the floodwaters that swamped New Orleans and now Galveston. He did not cause those things to happen. I'll tell you where God was, and is. God is there behind the police badges and in the fireman's suit. He is behind the scalpel and the syringe. He is there in the Coast Guard officials, the Marines, the Red Cross workers, the CERT teams, the Emergency Medical Technicians. He's there in the Salvation Army, in FEMA, in neighbors, in Governors, in Mayors, in nurses, in the President and, always, God is always near the heart of everyone who in the face of tragedy turns to God in repentance. God was there with all those who in these last few days, looked to Him, not for answers, but because in the end, tragedy taught them that we are mere mortals and fully dependent upon God.

You know, that's what Job did. He turned to God when everything he loved and cherished was taken from him. Job didn't blame God or curse Him, but instead, he praised Him. I am amazed every time I think about the story of Job. What was his secret, anyway? How could he respond in the way that he did?

Well, you see Job had learned how to separate those things that are temporary from those that are everlasting. He had learned how to separate those things he cherished and loved from, that which is eternal. He realized that all of his possessions and all of his earthly relationships were a gift of God, gifts that could only be enjoyed temporarily. Actually, the reason Job could praise God was because of a greater knowledge he possessed. There was something that he was able to cling to, something that could not be taken away from him. What was it? Well, listen to Job's words. He says: *"I know that my Redeemer lives, and that in the end He will stand upon the earth. And after my life has been destroyed, yet apart from my flesh I will see God; I will see Him with my own eyes, O how my heart yearns within me!"*[67] Job could praise God even though he had lost everything temporal, because of his faith in God, which gave him the hope he needed to hang on. He knew that God is eternal. He knew that his Redeemer would live forever. He knew that no matter what happened, he would one day see his Redeemer face to face. That's what got him through when he had lost everything this world can offer.

Job had been able to separate those things that were temporary from those things that were eternal before tragedy struck. And so when he did lose everything, he mourned, yes. But he did not as someone without hope. He knew that God was still with him. You know, we can make a list of all the things we hold dear. We can make a list of the temporal things of this earth we hold dear. A lot of people, I am sure, will have to do that over the next few days for insurance purposes. But, there is another very important list we need to think about, a list of that which is eternal.

First, as Christians, we, have salvation and eternal life. Jesus said: *"I am the resurrection and the life. He who believes in Me will live even though he dies; and whoever lives and believes in Me will never die."*[68] That is a promise that transcends physical death. And no one can destroy the relationship that exists between a believer and Jesus Christ. Jesus also said: *"My sheep listen to my voice; I know them, and they follow me. I give them eternal life, and they shall never perish; no one can snatch them out of my hand. My Father, who has given them to me, is greater than all; no one can snatch them out of my Father's hand."*[69] We may lose our physical dwelling here on earth and even our life, but we have an eternal home that Jesus has prepared for us, an eternal home and an eternal life that can never be destroyed. Jesus said: *"In My Father's house are many dwelling places; if it were not so would I have told you? I am going there to prepare a place for you. And if I go to prepare a place for you, I will come back and take you to be with Me that you also may be where I am."*[70]

Sooner or later, you and I will lose our earthly possessions and all the earthly relationships we hold dear, but if we have accepted Jesus Christ as our Savior, we have salvation and eternal life and a home in heaven that cannot be destroyed. So in light of that, what should we do when tragedy strikes? Well, first we should allow ourselves to mourn, as Job mourned. And second, with God's help, we should begin to rebuild. But, most importantly, we need to know that it was not God who brought about the tragedies. We can't blame God.

Now, some will still ask: If we can't blame it on God, who can we blame? Well, let me leave it at this. Blame it on the rain. Blame it on the wind. Blame it on our inadequacies. Blame it on the fact that creation and humankind fell in the Garden of Eden, but don't, blame it on God.

Where is God now? He is here, even in the midst of the suffering and despair. Anguish is no stranger to God. Let us never forget that Jesus suffered, He died. But, He was raised again. And because of that, even in the midst of tragedy, there is Hope, there is a way to rebuild, and because of His healing grace, there is a way that broken hearts and lives can be mended. Rely on His grace. After all, if God's grace can get us through the problem of fallen-ness, then it can get us through any other problem, as well. Rely on His grace. Amen.

The Upper Room

<u>Acts 9:32-42</u>
Now as Peter went here and there among all the believers, he came down also to the saints living in Lydda. There he found a man named Aeneas, who had been bedridden for eight years, for he was paralyzed. Peter said to him, "Aeneas, Jesus Christ heals you; get up and make your bed!" And immediately he got up. And all the residents of Lydda and Sharon saw him and turned to the Lord. Now in Joppa there was a disciple whose name was Tabitha, which in Greek is Dorcas. She was devoted to good works and acts of charity. At that time she became ill and died. When they had washed her, they laid her in a room upstairs. Since Lydda was near Joppa, the disciples, who heard that Peter was there, sent two men to him with the request, "Please come to us without delay." So Peter got up and went with them; and when he arrived, they took him to the room upstairs. All the widows stood beside him, weeping and showing tunics and other clothing that Dorcas had made while she was with them. Peter put all of them outside, and then he knelt down and prayed. He turned to the body and said, "Tabitha, get up." Then she opened her eyes, and seeing Peter, she sat up. He gave her his hand and helped her up. Then calling the saints and widows, he showed her to be alive. This became known throughout Joppa, and many believed in the Lord.

A king once was enjoying his garden while one of his counselors spoke of the wonderful works of God. "Show me a sign," said the king, "and I will believe." "Here are four acorns," said the counselor. "Will you, your Majesty, plant them in the ground and then stoop down and look into this clear pool of water?" The king did so. "Now," said the counselor, "look up."

The king looked up and saw four oak-trees where he had planted the acorns. "Wonderful!" he exclaimed, "This is indeed the work of God." "How long were you looking into the water," asked the counselor. "Only a second," said the king. "Eighty years have passed as a second," said the counselor. The king looked at his clothes; they were threadbare. He looked at his reflection in the water; he had become an old man. "This is no miracle," he said angrily. "Oh yes," said the counselor, "It is God's work, whether He did it in one second or eighty years."[71]

Miracles, in our scripture reading today, we hear of two miracles, the healing of a paralyzed man and the resuscitation of a woman whose body had been placed in the upper room to prepare it for burial. Upper room passages in the scriptures fascinate me. It seems that every time we hear about an upper room gathering, something amazing happens. I can think of three such times. The first was the night before Jesus was to be crucified. He instructed two of His disciples to go and prepare the Passover meal in an upper room that had already been set aside for the occasion. And there in that upper room Jesus shared with His disciples the most intimate details of His call and purpose. It was in there that He took bread which was considered to be a gift from God, and He blessed and broke it and gave it to His disciples. And said: *"Take, eat; this is My body."* Actually, the phrase, more clearly translated would be: *"This is myself."* It was Jesus' way of telling His followers that He would be present with them, even after He physically left this earth.

Jesus, in this upper room, is preparing His followers for His death, resurrection and return. And the next two gatherings will take place after He has risen from the dead. It was on the day of Pentecost that we hear about the second gathering. It was there that a miraculous indwelling of the power of the Holy Spirit took place, within the hearts of those present. This miraculous indwelling gave the early believers a boldness that they had not had before, a boldness to spread the good news of their Lord's resurrection.

You know, it is so easy to just sort of brush over passages like these, and to not see the miraculous changes that took place in those upper room experiences. And maybe that's because we are uncomfortable with the power of the Holy Spirit, uncomfortable because we can't really explain it completely. In this day of scientific reasoning we tend to want to deny that anything takes place that we can't explain. We are more comfortable saying that the miracles recorded by the early church didn't really happen. We want to explain them away, sort of sweep them under the rug, because, well, frankly they embarrass us. But, that really doesn't say a whole lot for our trust in God's Word, now does it? And, so, I want to take some time for us to think and to talk about the miracles recorded in there.

First a question, though. What is a miracle? Well, I think that we could probably agree that a miracle is an unexplainable event, that it is something we cannot figure out with our human minds. For example, we can't explain how God divided the Red Sea and allowed the Israelites to cross over on dry land. There was definitely some unexplainable power present. God performed many such miracles in the presence of His people: Not only did He divide the Red Sea for the fleeing Israelites. But, He also provided for them in the wilderness, causing manna to fall from heaven each morning to feed them. And in the dry land of the desert He caused water to flow out of a rock to quench the peoples' thirst. For forty years he provided for them and led them and showed His presence with them in a cloud by day and a pillar of fire by night.

There were many miracles that God performed during the Old Testament time. I could go on and on. But let's stop and ask: "Did God have a purpose? And if so, what was it?"

Well, each time a miracle took place God was demonstrating His power. Maybe that was His purpose, to show His people who was really in control. And it seemed to work. When Moses, their leader, had seen how God had miraculously provided for them he said: *Who is like You, O LORD, Who is like You, majestic in holiness, awesome in splendor, doing wonders? In Your steadfast love You led the people whom You redeemed; You guided them by Your strength to Your holy dwelling place.*[72] God performed miracles, I think, to demonstrate His power in the Old Testament. And in the New Testament we also see miracles being performed, as well, this time by God's Son: Jesus changed water into wine. He spoke to the raging winds and they became calm. He walked on water. He brought Lazarus back to life. He made the blind to see and healed the sick. He took a few loaves of bread and some fishes and fed five thousand people. And most importantly, He rose from the dead. Why did He do these things? Why did God allow all these miracles? Well, this time it was to show that Jesus was Messiah, that He was the Son of the living God: It was to show the world that He had control over life and death. It was to show the world that salvation and eternal life come through Him.

First, God performed miracles during the time of Israel. Then, Jesus, God the Son, performed miracles while He walked this earth in human form. And finally, after Jesus ascended into heaven His followers performed miracles in His name.

On one occasion Peter was in the village of Lydda where he found a man named Aeneas, a paralytic who had been bedridden for eight years, and he said to him: *Aeneas, Jesus Christ heals you; get up and make your bed! And immediately he got up. And all the residents of Lydda and Sharon saw him and they turned to the Lord.*[73]

And when a very devout disciple, a woman devoted to good works, named Tabitha or Dorcas in the Greek died, Peter went to Joppa where he: *Put all of the people outside, knelt down and prayed. And then turned to the body and said, Tabitha, get up. Then she opened her eyes, and seeing Peter, she sat up. He gave her his hand and helped her up. Then calling the saints and widows, Peter showed them that she was alive. This became known throughout Joppa, and many believed in the Lord.*[74] Peter and the others did these miraculous things in the power and name of Jesus Christ and because of the miracles, many believed.

Now we come to the present. Do miracles still happen today? Is God still in the miracle business? Well, think about it. We live in a world of miracles. There are many miracles that we take for granted, that we call natural events. Let me ask you: Why is the earth just the right distance from the sun so that we are warmed by it and get light from it yet we are not burned up by it? Why is it that the earth rotates to give us light from the sun by day and a pleasant darkness by night? Why is it when a farmer plants a seed in the earth it begins completely on its own to sprout and grow into a plant that provides food? And why is it that the leaves know to go up and the roots know to go down, even if the seed is planted upside down? Why do all these things happen with such precision? Aren't they things that we can't really explain scientifically? Oh, we can say that that's how it is, but can we say why? We, as mere human beings, have no control over these amazing things. But, someone does. And think about this. When you cut your hand you clean it up and maybe put a band-aid, or if it is really bad you go to the doctor and have stitches put in. But what happens? In a short time the skin begins to pull together and before you know it is healed. How does that happen? Isn't the healing we receive today as much of a miracle as the healing we read about in the Bible? In other words, ultimately, doesn't all healing come from God?

Several years ago, thirty doctors had very little hope that my son would live the night. But, miraculously he did. And he went into the medical journals as the first known person to survive the bacteria that had invaded his body. And like many of those first century believers, I too, witnessed a miracle. Even so, I am convinced that there is an even greater miracle then the one I observed nine years ago. And that is the miracle of a changed heart. Think about it, Saul, whose Greek name was Paul, was a killer of Christians. He witnessed and approved of the stoning of Stephen, the first Christian Martyr. Who could be worse than Saul? He murdered Christians, innocent Christians for their belief in Christ. Yet on a road to Damascus, through an experience with the divine, his life was turned completely around and miraculously changed. God worked powerfully in this man and because of his work many people have come to know the Lord. After Paul's conversion he said: *The saying is sure and worthy of full acceptance, that Christ Jesus came into the world to save sinners--of whom I am the foremost. But for that very reason I received mercy, so that in me, as the foremost sinner, Jesus Christ might display the utmost patience, making me an example to those who would come to believe in Him for eternal life.*[75]

Did you see it? Did you notice that even in the healing of Saul's heart, there was a purpose? God was able to use Paul's healed life as an example of God's awesome grace. Paul testifies to this, saying: *I received mercy, so that Jesus Christ would be able to use my conversion and my life as an example for those who would later believe in Christ.* You see, there was a purpose in Paul's conversion that was not only beneficial to Paul, but also, to others.

Through the Old Testament miracles God, revealed that He was the One in control. The New Testament miracles performed by Jesus pointed to the fact that He was Messiah, God the Son. And His followers, after His resurrection, also performed miracles in His name and many believed and, then in turn, they too told others about how God had come to dwell among us.

And even today in God's people, there is a purpose for God's miracles especially the miraculous conversion of a persons' heart. And that purpose is to use our lives as an example for those who will be watching us. The conversion of a persons' heart is the most important occurrence and the greatest miracle of all. It not only has a profound effect on a persons' life here on this earth, but also, throughout all of eternity. In essence, human life, life here on this earth and eternally, has no meaning until it discovers its reason for being. And that is why God continues to meet people in upper room experiences, offering the Bread from heaven, and giving the greatest gift of all, a relationship with Him. That's the business of our God.

You know, when we think of life, we think of a strong and healthy heart beating away inside our chest. But honestly, that's not all there is. A person cannot truly have "Life" until their heart beats true for Christ. A person cannot truly have "Life" until they have discovered their reason and purpose for being. What is your purpose here in this life? And how do you plan to live that out? If you're not sure, maybe you should take the words of Jesus more seriously when He says: *"Go to the place that I have designated for you and wait for the power from on high."*

For the first disciples that place was Jerusalem in an upper room. But, God has prepared upper rooms for us just the same. Actually, any place will do, if it's a quiet place where you can wait for the power of God. That's what the early believers did: They waited 50 days for the promised power from on high. That's what the saints and the widows, the friends of Tabitha, did: They waited there for Peter who was filled with the Holy Spirit to come. And they believed that he, through the power of that Spirit, would be able to perform a miracle. And then they received that same power, that same boldness and *"made it known throughout all Joppa, and many more believed."*[76]

Do you see the pattern here? God has a pattern and a purpose. First, there is a desire to experience Life, true Life in the Spirit of Christ. Second, there is a time of waiting. Third, the promise is fulfilled as the power is given. And finally, there is a going out to share the good news with others. Desire, Waiting, Receiving, Going out, that's what Life, true Life in Christ is all about.

Do you have that Life? Have you received that power? Do you have the boldness that comes from a vibrant, active Life with Christ? Right now, I am going to ask our pianist to play some soft music as we take a few moments to *"go to the place that Jesus has designated for us today and ask God for His promised power from on high."* Let us now take a few moments in silent prayer.

What Is Important?

Matthew 21:23-32
When he entered the temple, the chief priests and the elders of the people came to him as he was teaching, and said, "By what authority are you doing these things, and who gave you this authority?" Jesus said to them, "I will also ask you one question; if you tell me the answer, then I will also tell you by what authority I do these things. Did the baptism of John come from heaven, or was it of human origin?" And they argued with one another, "If we say, 'From heaven,' he will say to us, 'Why then did you not believe him?' But if we say, 'Of human origin,' we are afraid of the crowd; for all regard John as a prophet." So they answered Jesus, "We do not know." And he said to them, "Neither will I tell you by what authority I am doing these things. "What do you think? A man had two sons; he went to the first and said, 'Son, go and work in the vineyard today.' He answered, 'I will not'; but later he changed his mind and went. The father went to the second and said the same; and he answered, 'I go, sir'; but he did not go. Which of the two did the will of his father?" They said, "The first." Jesus said to them, "Truly I tell you, the tax collectors and the prostitutes are going into the kingdom of God ahead of you. For John came to you in the way of righteousness and you did not believe him, but the tax collectors and the prostitutes believed him; and even after you saw it, you did not change your minds and believe him.

There is a great story about a group of military leaders who built a super computer that was supposed to be able to solve any problem. These leaders gathered in front of the new machine for a demonstration. The engineer there with them instructed them to feed a difficult problem into the computer. The generals proceeded to describe a hypothetical situation to the computer and then asked the pivotal question: Attack or retreat?

And the enormous super computer hummed away for an hour and then printed out its one-word answer: Yes. The generals looked at each other, somewhat confused. Finally one of them submitted a second question to the computer: Yes what? Instantly the computer responded: Yes, Sir!

Now, the Pharisees, like the generals, were accustomed to people saying "Yes, sir" to them. They were the religious authorities and they were used to being treated as such. But now, there was a new teacher in town, a teacher who was threatening their authority. And the Pharisees were alarmed. They feared Jesus' popularity and His ability to heal and perform miracles. In their eyes, Jesus was preaching heresy and leading people away from the traditions that defined the Jewish religion. And they wanted to expose Jesus as a fraud. So, they decided to try to incriminate Him by asking Him a two-part question: *"By what authority are you doing these things, and who gave you this authority?"* It was an obvious trap and knowing that, Jesus countered with a two-part question of His own. He asked: *"Did the baptism of John come from heaven, or was it of human origin?"* And realizing that this was a no-win situation, the Pharisees finally said: *"We do not know."* And Jesus said: *Well, then neither will I tell you from where my authority comes.*

Let us pray: May the words of my mouth and the meditations of each of our hearts be acceptable in Your sight, O God, our Rock and our Redeemer. Amen.

You know, sometimes we are blind to what God is doing in our midst. And that was certainly true of the religious leaders that day when Jesus stood among them. He was standing right in front of them and they failed to recognize Him as God's own Son. So, Jesus tells a story, possibly to shock them out of their complacency. *"There were two sons,"* He said. The father told each one to go and do a little work in the vineyard.

And as the story goes, the first son said: *"I won't go."* But afterwards, he changes his mind and goes to work anyway. Later the second son said: *"All right, sir, I'll go"* but he never went near the vineyard. Which of these two, Jesus asked, did what the father wanted? Well, the second son had good intensions. He didn't rebel when his father asked him to work in the field. He didn't talk back to him. He must have had good intentions. But, which of these two did what the father wanted? Was it the one with good intentions? Well, no. That son never made it to the vineyard. But, the first son, at first saying no, finally did go and do the work in the vineyard. He changed his mind and went obediently and did the work his father asked him to do. And after Jesus told this story, He then said to the Pharisees: *I tell you the truth, the tax collectors and the prostitutes are entering the kingdom of God ahead of you.*

What did He mean by that? Well, you see, the Kingdom of God is not simply some far off, future reward although it does extend into eternity, but it is also something that begins in this life. And so the prostitutes and tax collectors had already begun to experience the kingdom because of their belief that Jesus was the Christ. Evidently, belief in the fact that Jesus was who John the Baptist said He was, was important to them. Unlike the Pharisees, the tax collectors and prostitutes were aware of their need for forgiveness, and they accepted Jesus as the Messiah immediately.

What it all boils down to is the question, of what is truly important in life: Is having authority over others important? Is the image of always being right and never being wrong important? Is enjoying a certain status in this life important? Is it a certain level of popularity, or living in a certain neighborhood, or having the newest, most expensive car or house that's important? What is truly important? That is a question we all have to deal with at some point in our lives. Over these past several weeks, more than a few folks have had to try and answer that question, after the devastation of Hurricane Ike.

Lots of people recently have been forced to think about what is truly important. Did you hear about the family who had just recently, bought a new home in Galveston? Just before the hurricane, they closed on their new home, which was then completely destroyed by Ike. Now, don't you know that they had to ask the question: What is truly important in this life, among other things? If you have listened to the news lately you know of all of the devastation and difficulties in the wake of hurricane Ike. But contrast that picture with a newspaper article about a businessman, a contractor, whose specialty was homes for the super rich.

The article talked about a plywood box that contained a 5,000 pound antique bathtub carved from a single block of marble which would sit in the master bathroom of a $7,000,000 home. The builder went on to say that that was nothing unusual - thousand-dollar door hinges, $10,000 gold-plated faucets, custom-made cabinets, even in the laundry room, are common in homes like those. But don't you think we might have to ask: How valuable any house would really be, if it was in the path of a hurricane or a tornado? Good question. I mean how valuable would a 5000 pound, antique marble bathtub carved from a single block of stone be if it was cracked into pieces and washed into one of those huge piles of rubble we've seen lately in Galveston or Houston? Jesus once said: *"Do not store up for yourselves treasures on earth, where moth and rust consume and where thieves break in and steal,"* or we might add where it floats away in a flood or is left behind in an evacuation. *"But store up for yourselves treasures in heaven, where neither moth nor rust consumes and where thieves do not break in and steal. For where your treasure is, there your heart will be also."*

After a devastating Hurricane in 1999, hurricane Floyd, one pastor wrote about her ordeal, as she was forced to quickly evacuate her home. Listen to how she closes her story. She writes: All in all it was quite an experience and very important in a way for me. Now, I really know what matters most. It is my family and my friends and my God. It is helping people in need.

It is the sharing of resources with others. It is a good bed and shelter and food. I will be fine in any situation if I think vertically. Every material thing I have is, after all, simply "a thing" that can be replaced. Things can be replaced, but human life is different. It should never be wasted. And no talent given by God should ever be hidden or go un-used. Compassion and prayer for example, she said are healing gifts and they are ours to give in every situation.[77] Sometimes it takes an event like Floyd or Katrina or Rita or Ike to help us put things in perspective, doesn't it? Sometimes it takes things like that to help us sort the wheat from the chaff in the jumble of our lives, to help us see what is truly important.

On one occasion there were two men talking about the death of a rich neighbor of theirs. The first man asked the other, "How much did he leave behind?" And the second man responded: "Well, all of it." I wonder what was truly important to the first man, who was concerned with the material riches of his neighbor. And I also wonder what was truly important to the second son in Jesus' story who was too busy with "life and things" to do what his father asked him to do. The question about "what is truly important in this life," is not new by any means. I think that the first son, the one who did work in his father's vineyard, must have asked himself that same question and decided, that it was his relationship with his father that was the most important.

Jesus once said: *"Do not worry about the things of this world. God knows what you need and will provide for you just as the birds of the air are fed and the lilies of the field are dressed."* And if God will take care of the birds and flowers, well think about how He will take care of you. Basically, Jesus says: If you are going to be concerned with anything, it should be with, that of making sure that the things that are important to you are also the things that are important to God. *"Seek ye first the Kingdom of God and His righteousness, and all these things shall be added unto you,"* Jesus says.[78]

In the last few weeks, we have been reminded too graphically, I think, that "things" can be gone in a flash, or in a flash flood. So it's a good thing to remember Jesus' words of wisdom when He says: *Make God's priorities your priorities,* then everything else will come together for you as God provides. Making God's priorities your priorities, while holding loosely to the material things of this world, seeking God's will in how you might best work in His vineyard, and trusting in His awesome provision. Spiritual things, it is the spiritual things of life, that our Lord would say are of the utmost importance. Everything else will fade away, and will eventually pass into another's hands. We are only stewards of the material things God provides for us in this life. But, when it comes to spiritual things, like love for God and a willingness to serve Him, well, those are the things that will last throughout eternity. What you choose to do for God in this lifetime, will last throughout eternity. Now that's amazing. Just think on that, for a while. Amen.

Wedding Attire

Matthew 22:1-14

Once more Jesus spoke to them in parables, saying: "The kingdom of heaven may be compared to a king who gave a wedding banquet for his son. He sent his slaves to call those who had been invited to the wedding banquet, but they would not come. Again he sent other slaves, saying, 'Tell those who have been invited: Look, I have prepared my dinner, my oxen and my fat calves have been slaughtered, and everything is ready; come to the wedding banquet.' But they made light of it and went away, one to his farm, another to his business, while the rest seized his slaves, mistreated them, and killed them. The king was enraged. He sent his troops, destroyed those murderers, and burned their city. Then he said to his slaves, 'The wedding is ready, but those invited were not worthy. Go therefore into the main streets, and invite everyone you find to the wedding banquet.' Those slaves went out into the streets and gathered all whom they found, both good and bad; so the wedding hall was filled with guests. "But when the king came in to see the guests, he noticed a man there who was not wearing a wedding robe, and he said to him, 'Friend, how did you get in here without a wedding robe?' And he was speechless. Then the king said to the attendants, 'Bind him hand and foot, and throw him into the outer darkness, where there will be weeping and gnashing of teeth.' For many are called, but few are chosen."

Perhaps you have heard of the family that moved into the neighborhood and the little country church decided to reach out to them. When they arrived at the house the members of the church were surprised to find that the family had 12 kids and were very poor. They invited the family to worship and then said goodbye.

Later that week the church delivered a package to the family and said: "We want you to know that y'all are welcome at our church anytime. We have bought you these gifts and hope you will feel comfortable in our congregation." And they left. The family opened the package to find 14 suits of clothing, beautiful clothes for every member of the family. Sunday came and the people waited for the family to arrive. But, the family never showed. Wondering what could have possibly happened, the church members returned to the new family's home after worship, and found them just getting back, all dressed in their new clothes. "We don't mean to be nosey," they said, "but we were wondering what happened. We had hoped to see you this morning in church." And the father spoke up, saying: "Well, we got up this morning intending to come. And we sure do appreciate your invitation. But after we showered and dressed, why, we looked so proper that we went to the Episcopal Church." This morning we will be talking about the proper attire for a King's banquet.

Let us pray: May the words of my mouth and the meditations of each of our hearts be acceptable in Your sight, O God, our Rock and our Redeemer. Amen.

In our parable this morning, the first thing we notice is that everyone is invited to the king's reception. We also notice that the original invited wedding guests, the ones invited, not just once, but twice, were God's beloved people, Israel. Historically and spiritually, they should have been the first to say "yes." They were the people who knew the true God and who, along with their ancestors, longed for the Bridegroom, Israel's Messiah.

The first thing we notice in this parable is that everyone is invited to the king's reception. And the second thing we notice is that not everyone responds in a positive way. Some made excuses about why they could not attend.

I like the way the Gospel of Luke records the excuses. He gives us more details about them. "They all began to make excuses," he writes, saying: I have just bought a field, and I must go and see it. Please excuse me, one said. I have just bought five yoke of oxen, and I'm on my way to try them out. Please excuse me, another said. The last one said: I just got married, so I can't come.

What was it that kept these people from the feast? Well, it wasn't because of bad feelings toward the host. Apparently it had nothing to do with him. They were sorry, but they were busy. They were preoccupied. It seemed that they were kept away by business and family ties. And what's so bad about that? What is wrong with purchasing land? What is wrong with checking out a business investment? What, indeed, is wrong with getting married? Well, the point our Lord is making in is that even good things can be, and often are, the enemy of the best. A person doesn't have to do wrong things or even shallow things to miss the Kingdom. He or she need only be too preoccupied with things that will keep their mind off the Kingdom. That's why Jesus so often warned us about material possessions and family ties. He saw how absorbing they can be, completely using up a person's thoughts and affections, so that there is nothing left over for the higher things in life. He didn't mean that everyone must renounce business and family to follow God although some have felt called to a vow of poverty or celibacy. But He did mean that a person must keep the claims of God's Kingdom first in his or her life, having a right sense of value and discernment, is what is important here.

It was excessive preoccupation with business and family that kept these people out of the Kingdom. They used those things as an excuse, and it seems to me that they really had no true desire to go. If they had wanted to go badly enough they could have managed. You know, it is really amazing how quickly people can clear their calendars to do the things that they want to do? But these guests just let other commitments keep them from the kingdom festival.

One of the greatest enemies of faith and salvation even to this day is preoccupation, where God is simply crowded out. The most common complaint about life, is that there is simply not enough time in the day. A young wife called the food editor of a local newspaper office. "Would you please help me?" she asked. "I'm cooking a special dinner tonight for my husband's boss and his wife. I've never cooked a big dinner before, and I want everything to be perfect. I bought a nine-pound turkey. Could you tell me how long to cook it in my new microwave?" "Just a minute," the food editor said, as he turned to check his reference book. "Oh, a minute?" she exclaimed. Thank you. You've been a big help." And she hung up.[79]

The most common complaint about life is that there is simply not enough time in the day. An executive with a telegraph company went traveling one day. It was extremely cold outside when he arrived at the bus station and went into the local telegraph office hoping to get warm. When he got inside, however, it was cold. He noticed there was no fire in the fireplace. He said to the young telegraph operator, "Why don't you build a fire in this place and warm it up?" The young man said: "Listen mister, I'm too busy sending telegrams to build fires." The man then told the boy that he was the vice-president of the company and that he wanted him to send a telegram to the home office at once. The message was: "Fire this man immediately." A moment later the young man went out to get a load of wood so he could build a fire. The executive asked: "Young man, have you sent that telegram yet?" And he responded: "Listen mister, I'm too busy building fires to send telegrams."[80]

The point is this. We have to decide what really matters in life and the try to make the right choices. Time with our family, service in our community, attention to our work, self-improvement, these are all important. But the most important thing is time with God. If God is not at the very top of our list, everything else that is important to us will eventually crumble.

If you have put other things, important as they may be, ahead of God, then you are running the risk of being too preoccupied and missing the banquet, altogether. In other words: If you are too busy to respond to God's voice, then you are too busy. If you are too busy to use your God given gifts for His Kingdom, then you are too busy. One day our relationship with God will be the only priority that will matter. And if we keep putting our relationship with Him on the back burner, we could wait too long and find ourselves outside the banquet.

The great enemy of faith is that of preoccupation. It's not that we disbelieve in God. Nor do we despise Him. Not really. We simply have no time for Him. We are not irreligious. We're just busy and we are tired. Other matters are pressing, and we feel that heaven can wait. But, can it really?

First, all are invited to the kings' banquet. Second, few will respond. And finally, it is the King, in the end, who will choose who can stay. You see, Jesus is warning us that we must be properly prepared; we must be properly dressed for the occasion. Jesus is warning us about the importance of being prepared, properly attired for the summons of God. You and I are invited to be His kingdom guests. Because of our relationship with Jesus Christ, our names are on God's guest list. But, will we truly enter into this wedding feast? Jesus' own words were: *"Many are called, but few are chosen."* Will we truly enter into the matter of salvation, with hearts and lives willing to be changed and transformed for Christ?

Are you properly dressed for the wedding party? Are you clothed in things like: A pure heart, a generous spirit, a life of obedience? Are you ready for the wedding feast?

A cute story appeared in a Christian magazine a few years ago. You probably have heard it. It goes like this. A woman took her four-year-old granddaughter to the doctor's office with a fever. The doctor looked in her ears and said, "Who's in there? Donald Duck?" And the little girl said: "No."

He looked in her mouth and said, "Who's in there? Mickey Mouse?" Again she said: "No." Then he listened to her heart with the stethoscope and said, "Who's in there? Barney?" And she replied: "No, Jesus is in my heart. Barney is on my underwear."[81] According to this young Christian, what really mattered was that Jesus was in her heart. But, the more mature Christian will also be concerned about the outer attire. What about the fruit of the Christian life? What about Faith, Hope, Love, Forgiveness, Tolerance, Obedience and all the other virtues that are evidence of a transformed life? What about your outer attire. What will you be wearing to the king's reception?

The first and second invitations have already gone out. The time has come. Will you be properly dressed? Will you be properly prepared? Let me suggest, in the words of the Apostle Paul, that you *"clothe yourself in Christ,* now, in this life, today. So when the time does come, when the final victory feast does begin, you will be among "the few" who are "chosen" by our Lord. Clothe yourself in the proper wedding attire. Clothe yourself in Christ. Amen.

Salvation... It is Now!

Matthew 8:1-17

When Jesus had come down from the mountain, great crowds followed him; and there was a leper who came to him and knelt before him, saying, "Lord, if you choose, you can make me clean." He stretched out his hand and touched him, saying, "I do choose. Be made clean!" Immediately his leprosy was cleansed. Then Jesus said to him, "See that you say nothing to anyone; but go, show yourself to the priest, and offer the gift that Moses commanded, as a testimony to them." When he entered Capernaum, a centurion came to him, appealing to him and saying, "Lord, my servant is lying at home paralyzed, in terrible distress." And he said to him, "I will come and cure him." The centurion answered, "Lord, I am not worthy to have you come under my roof; but only speak the word, and my servant will be healed. For I also am a man under authority, with soldiers under me; and I say to one, 'Go,' and he goes, and to another, 'Come,' and he comes, and to my slave, 'Do this,' and the slave does it." When Jesus heard him, he was amazed and said to those who followed him, "Truly I tell you, in no one in Israel have I found such faith. I tell you, many will come from east and west and will eat with Abraham and Isaac and Jacob in the kingdom of heaven, while the heirs of the kingdom will be thrown into the outer darkness, where there will be weeping and gnashing of teeth." And to the centurion Jesus said, "Go; let it be done for you according to your faith." And the servant was healed in that hour. When Jesus entered Peter's house, he saw his mother-in-law lying in bed with a fever; he touched her hand, and the fever left her, and she got up and began to serve him. That evening they brought to him many who were possessed with demons; and he cast out the spirits with a word, and cured all who were sick. This was to fulfill what had been spoken through the prophet Isaiah, "He took our infirmities and bore our diseases."

Satan once called a meeting to devise a plan to get people to reject the Good News of salvation. "Let's go to them and say there is no God," proposed one. But silence prevailed, because all knew that most people believed in God. "Let's tell them there is no hell, no future punishment for the wicked," offered another. That was turned down, too, because they couldn't imagine people not believing in hell. The meeting was just about to end in failure when there came a voice from the back of the room: "Tell them there is a God, there is a hell and that the Bible is the Word of God. But then tell them there is plenty of time to make their decision for Christ." All hell erupted with ghoulish glee, for they knew that if a person procrastinated on receiving Christ, they usually never accepted Him. Then they all went out to deceive as many people as they could.[82] Today we are going to talk about Salvation which begins when a person believes in Jesus Christ and all He's done.

Let us pray: May the words of my mouth and the meditations of each of our hearts be acceptable in Your sight, O God, our Rock and our Redeemer. Amen.

Salvation, what does it mean to be saved? Well, in traditional terms, Jesus saves us from personal sin and the consequences of original sin. But that's not all. Jesus says to those He comes in contact with: *The Kingdom of God is near.*[83]

Most of us believe that Jesus came to heal our souls and take away our sin, but how are we doing with the concept that Jesus came to heal sicknesses of the body? We struggle with that because, physical illness is sometimes, wrongfully presented, not as an evil, but as something desired by God for some reason beyond our grasp. Actually, the question most asked is this: Is it God's will that we be sick or is it God's will that we enjoy good health? Well, according to the New Testament, every time Jesus met with evil whether it was spiritual or physical, He treated it as an enemy. When a sick person came to Him in faith, Jesus healed that person, pure and simple.

He didn't divide people into a soul to be saved and a body that is to suffer and remain unhealed until the time when the last trumpet sounds and all who are in Christ will rise to receive their resurrection bodies. No, even in this life, over and over again Jesus healed people, both spiritually and physically.

Happily, we sometimes get a glimpse of the Good News even today, that salvation is for the whole person, that salvation means fullness of life in every possible way, and that wholeness of mind, body and spirit is God's desire for us. Matthew's Gospel reflects this understanding, as he writes about a day in the life of Jesus. This gospel writer tells us: That on a particular day, Jesus first cures a leper, then heals a centurion's servant and finally cures Peter's mother-in-law of a fever. And then he tells us what happened in response to the good work Jesus has done. He writes: *That evening they brought to Jesus many who were possessed with demons; and He cast out the spirits with a word, and cured all who were sick. This was to fulfill what had been spoken through the prophet Isaiah, "He took our infirmities and bore our diseases."*[84] Now, not only did Jesus evangelize by healing the sick and casting out evil spirits, but He also instructed His disciples to do the same.[85] That's what the first Christians did. But, after about 400 years or so, something happened and our belief in divine healing began to decline.

Why? Well, I think there are two main reasons. First, it seems that there was a misguided philosophy that began to creep into the Christian belief system sometime in the latter part of the first century, that of a duality of body and soul. It was a philosophy that wrongly stated that the spirit is good and the body bad, that the human soul is somehow imprisoned in an evil body and that it longs to be released.

This, of course, is not what Jesus taught or modeled for us. Goodness of body goes all the way back to the Garden of Eden, where God, on the sixth day said: *Let us make humankind in our image, according to our likeness, So God created humankind in His image, in the image of God He created them; male and female He created them. And God saw everything that He had made, and indeed, it was very good.*[86]

The second thing I feel holds modern day Christians back from believing in the power of healing prayer, is a misinterpretation of Jesus' teaching on suffering. Let's take a look at that. First of all, the cross that Jesus carried was a cross of persecution. His suffering came from the outside, through the wickedness of people who allowed evil to rule in their lives. Jesus suffered deeply, but the source of His anguish came from outside of Himself. And, most importantly, notice the suffering Jesus did not endure, and even took away from those who approached Him in faith, that of sickness. Jesus did suffer, and He told his followers to *"carry their own cross, daily."* But nowhere in the Bible do we find that Jesus suffered with physical illness. No, instead, Jesus enjoyed wholeness, in all the areas of emotional, physical and spiritual health. And Jesus, Himself, distinguished between sickness and persecution. He told His disciples that they would be: *Persecuted, hauled before magistrates and judges, thrown out of the synagogues, that their enemies would be their own brothers and sisters and that they should rejoice when all manner of evil was spoken about them.*[87] But He was never seen counseling a sick person to rejoice or to be patient because disease would be helpful or redemptive; but instead Jesus *"cured them all."*[88]

Okay, so what do we do with the suffering and illnesses that we experience? Well, certainly, there is no simple answer, but here are a few ideas that may help. First, the glory of God is a human being fully alive. God has revealed Himself as being on the side of life; He is life. God has revealed Himself as being on the side of life, of wholeness, and of health in mind, body and spirit. So, in general, it is God's desire that we be healthy rather than sick.

Second, sickness is in and of itself an evil. Sickness is ordinarily not directly willed by God but it is part of our fallen human condition. Third, there will come a time for each of us to die. Even, Lazarus, who Jesus raised from the dead, later died. But consider this. It is normal for an apple to drop to the ground in the autumn after it has spent the summer ripening to its fullness and growth. But it is not normal for a green apple to fall off the tree in July because a worm has gotten into it. When that happens, then something has gone wrong.

Finally, some sicknesses may, indeed, have a higher purpose. Remember Paul, who was blinded on his way to Damascus, and during that time met the Lord who completely changed his life? His blindness lasted three days until he was healed by the prayer of Annanias. Another time, he fell sick in Galatia, which gave him the chance to preach the Good News to the people there.[89] But notice, on each occasion Paul does recover. It is just a fact that, the glory of God is a human being fully alive, a whole and healthy human being in mind, body and spirit.

Today, we heard that Jesus came down a mountain, and then a leper came to Him, saying: *"Lord, if You will, You can make me clean."* And Jesus stretched out His hand and touched him and he was clean. Later, He met a Roman centurion who asked Jesus to heal his servant. Jesus marveled at this man's faith, and said: *"Go; it has been done for you because you have believed."*[90] Then Jesus went to Simon Peter's house where He discovered that Simon's mother-in-law was sick with a high fever. He simply touched her and the fever left her. Over and over again, the biblical text speaks of the healing touch of Jesus. And so, we discover that it is very simple, and simply this: Jesus responds to the human situation; He responds to the human need. The touch of His hand cures us. Sometimes it is a physical illness.

There are many examples, even today, of people who have been healed of some physical illness when the doctors saw no cure. My son is among them. I was one of those parents who heard, first hand: "Your son's healing has come from a higher source." Sometimes it is a physical illness. Sometimes it is an emotional illness, an illness of the mind, where only the touch of God can heal a person. Sometimes it is an illness in relationships. The headlines are full of it every day: strife between nations, groups, classes, races, families and individuals. And, of course, it could be a spiritual illness where a person needs to surrender his or her life to the Lord. Whatever it is, all of us live all the time in a danger zone, in a danger zone of possibly experiencing illness, in mind, body or spirit. And when that happens, we need to remember the words Jesus spoke to those He came in contact with, He said to them: *"The Kingdom of God is near, repent and believe in the Good News."*[91]

Have you opened your life to the touch of the Master's hand? Have you sought out the fullness of God's Salvation which is now among us, which begins now and continues into eternity?

Right now, all are invited to come forward to the kneeling rail, so as to seek God's healing in your life. Please come, today is God's day for full Salvation!

Would You Be A Saint?

Matthew 23:1-12
Then Jesus said to the crowds and to his disciples, "The scribes and the Pharisees sit on Moses' seat; therefore, do whatever they teach you and follow it; but do not do as they do, for they do not practice what they teach. They tie up heavy burdens, hard to bear, and lay them on the shoulders of others; but they themselves are unwilling to lift a finger to move them. They do all their deeds to be seen by others; for they make their phylacteries broad and their fringes long. They love to have the place of honor at banquets and the best seats in the synagogues, and to be greeted with respect in the marketplaces, and to have people call them rabbi. But you are not to be called rabbi, for you have one teacher, and you are all students. And call no one your father on earth, for you have one Father-- the one in heaven. Nor are you to be called instructors, for you have one instructor, the Messiah. The greatest among you will be your servant. All who exalt themselves will be humbled, and all who humble themselves will be exalted.

How many of you played "dress up" this weekend? Wow, well, I thought we would have at least one. On Halloween people "dress up" in costumes and put on masks to "hide out," to conceal who they really are. Originally the "disguises" worn on "All Hallows Eve" were supposed to fool the demons and other dark forces roaming the earth on that fateful night. The idea was that good Christians would be left alone by evil spirits if they dressed to look like they themselves were part of Satan's army.

My, oh my, how times have changed. I don't think too many demons were put-off by Barbie Princesses, High School Musical cheerleaders, or Star Wars soldiers. No, times have changed. A lot of people dressed up on Friday night. But for a lot of Christians the "dressing up" in costume didn't stop with Friday night. They also "dressed up" to come to church this morning. They exchanged their Friday night "sinner" for their Sunday "saint" costume.

You know, for some reason many of us have become convinced that there is somehow a connection between what we wear on the outside, our clothing, and what we wear on the inside, our spiritual condition. But, really, the family, the Body of Christ, is more complex than that. And this complexity is what makes this "Christ-Body" so vital. You see, both Saints and Sinners are present and accounted for, because all of us are both. The writer of John attests to this when he writes the words of Jesus spoken to the accusers of a woman caught in adultery, saying: *"Let anyone among you who is without sin be the first to throw a stone at her." And they all went away, one by one.* Then Jesus continued, saying to the woman: *"Where are they? Has no one condemned you?" And she said, "No one, sir." And Jesus said, "Neither do I condemn you. Go your way, and from now on do not sin again."*[92]

The fact of the matter is this: we are both Saints and sinners. Jesus knew that when He encouraged this woman to *"go and sin no more."* God's desire for us, of course, is to be completely sanctified Saints, but right now, in this lifetime, well, it seems that we, even in the church, are just a work in process.

Now, over the years, from time to time, someone may have asked you something like this: "Would you be a saint and bring me that sweater?" Or maybe, "Would you be a saint and do the dishes while I'm gone?" And it is requests like these that give us opportunity to register ourselves as "saints." But, is that all there is to being a "saint" or is there some deeper commitment, something greater required of a "saint?"

We all know there are true saints in our midst this morning. Can't you feel their presence? Every Lord's Day, every Sunday we recognize and celebrate them. But here is our problem. The problem with real living "saints" is that they are slippery. Jesus identified the qualities of a true living "saint" of His day. They don't flaunt their achievements. They do not wear "broad phylacteries" or "long fringes." They do not insist upon having the best, they don't need to be recognized for their deeds, they don't ask for special placement in the community or the best seats in the sanctuary. No, true living "saints" slip under the radar most of the time. And so, it just takes time and effort to find those "real" saints, who are among us. Like: Those who give without expectation, those who love without reservation, or those who sacrifice without expecting anything in return. People who give, love, and sacrifice, without ever asking for recognition or recompense, are those who qualify as living "saints" within the Body of Christ, today.

Yesterday was "All Saints Day" and so, that makes today "All Saints Sunday." It is the one day we make a concerted effort to recognize and celebrate all the "saints," some of who have been gone for centuries, whose legacy of love continues on, saints like St. Paul, St. Augustine, St. Francis, St. Theresa, St. Jerome, and all the saints appropriately identified and honored by the big "capital C" Church. But there are also our local saints among us. And they don't have to be utterly without sin. That is a far cry from the biblical standard of a saint. St. Peter denied Christ three times. St. Paul persecuted Christians and cheered at Stephen's stoning. St. Augustine was spoiled, promiscuous and rebellious as a youth. St. Aquinas was gluttonous, rude, and abusive. Even as we read in the Bible, in Hebrews 11, the great "communion of saints" chapter, we can't find one person listed in that "communion" that is without some kind of imperfection. Why, well because every Christian "saint" first comes to us as a "sinner." That's why, in the Bible we see imperfect saints.

Okay, the way we play on Halloween is by putting on a mask, pretending to be something we are not. But, the way Christians reclaim their identity on All Saints Day is by stripping off those masks. We expose who we really are, what we really care about, and who we really love, and we do that by removing our masks. If All Hallows' Eve is all about Masking, All Saints Day is all about Unmasking, unmasking the saints. Because saints don't wear masks: Saints do wear, however, their hearts on their sleeves. Saints do wear weariness in well doing. Saints do wear crowns of suffering and long-suffering (patience). Saints do wear crowns of martyrdom sometimes. Saints do these things, because saints always love.

Today we celebrate all those saints who stand in our midst. Living "saints" are those people who keep the heart of the Body of Christ beating, who keep the Body of Christ warm, vital, and alive, for the whole world to see. I saw a whole bunch of them at the Emmaus gathering yesterday evening in Brenham.

You know, I think it's time that we lift up the saints in our midst. In fact, maybe we need to reframe that word saint, since it is such a sterile, cold word. Let's change the word "saint" to "a real human person." The person who cleans the bathrooms before church on Sunday is a real human person, a saint. The parent or grandparent who takes three or four extra kids home from an event because they can, is a real human person, a saint. The retiree who volunteers time with children or teenagers or gets up at three in the morning to go out and help to give flu shots, is a real human person, a saint. The number cruncher who spends a lifetime balancing budgets and then spends their "down-time" helping un-scramble church finances, is a real human person, a saint.

There are potential saints everywhere. Maybe we need to speak some more of these saints into existence. The grocery store checker who makes sure your eggs aren't cracked and asks if everything is okay, is a saint! The bank-teller who looks you in the eye and notes it is a beautiful day, is a saint! The driver who lets you go first at the four way stop, is a saint.

"Those who exalt themselves will be humbled, and all who humble themselves will be exalted," Jesus promises. Saints are not those who exceed all the rest of us. Saints are those who most wholly manifest Jesus' teaching on service and self-giving sacrifice. The true saint is not a non-sinner. The true saint is one who humbles him or herself in obedience to Christ, serving others, while, at the same time, not concerning themselves with what they might receive in return. These are just some of the saints among us. I'm sure you could name more.

So here's the bottom line, here's the question for you to take away with you this morning: Would YOU, be a saint? Or maybe better reframed: Would you BE, a saint? I encourage you to ponder this question as you come forward for Holy Communion, today. Amen.

Some Are Wise

<u>Matthew 25:1-13</u>
"Then the kingdom of heaven will be like this. Ten bridesmaids took their lamps and went to meet the bridegroom. Five of them were foolish, and five were wise. When the foolish took their lamps, they took no oil with them; but the wise took flasks of oil with their lamps. As the bridegroom was delayed, all of them became drowsy and slept. But at midnight there was a shout, 'Look! Here is the bridegroom! Come out to meet him.' Then all those bridesmaids got up and trimmed their lamps. The foolish said to the wise, 'Give us some of your oil, for our lamps are going out.' But the wise replied, 'No! there will not be enough for you and for us; you had better go to the dealers and buy some for yourselves.' And while they went to buy it, the bridegroom came, and those who were ready went with him into the wedding banquet; and the door was shut. Later the other bridesmaids came also, saying, 'Lord, lord, open to us.' But he replied, 'Truly I tell you, I do not know you.' Keep awake therefore, for you know neither the day nor the hour.

On several occasions Jesus taught about what it means to be wise. And we find three in the Gospel of Matthew alone. The first was when Jesus told the parable about a wise man who built his house upon rock.[93] The second was about a wise slave who was found to be doing the Master's work when He returned.[94] And the third was about five wise bridesmaids who were ready for the Bridegroom's return. The acquirement of wisdom was important to Jesus, and so it ought to be important to us, as well. That's what our subject will be today.

Let us pray: May the words of my mouth and the meditations of each of our hearts be acceptable in Your sight, O God, our Rock and our Redeemer. Amen.

A well known biblical scholar, teacher and preacher once said: Wisdom comes privately from God as a person applies spiritual principles to daily life.[95] But, how do we make right decisions? How do we actually go about applying spiritual principles? How do we build our house upon rock and not sand? How can we be faithful servants when the Master returns? And what was it about those five wise bridesmaids who joyfully went into the wedding banquet that day?

Well, maybe their joy tied in somehow to the list found earlier in the Gospel of Matthew, the list that came from Jesus' teaching on the Beatitudes. Jesus says: Those who know their lives are not their own, those who lament over the present condition of this world, those who renounce violence, those who long for a time when everything will be right before God, those who are merciful, those who are devoted to God, those who seek reconciliation with God and others, as far as it is possible, and finally, those who are persecuted for their obedience to Christ, will be blessed.[96] Maybe these were some of the qualities that the five wise and joyful bridesmaids possessed that day.

In our reading, we hear that there are ten bridesmaids, but that only five of them are blessed as they are allowed to enter into the wedding banquet. All ten come to the wedding; all ten in the beginning have their lamps aglow with expectation and all ten, presumably, have on their long gowns. But it isn't because of any of these things that they are set apart; no it's because of something else. It's because of the fact that some have enough "oil" to wait for the wedding banquet, even when it is delayed.

All ten bridesmaids have "lamps" (let's call that their faith, they all have faith) but only five of them have enough "oil" to sustain their faithfulness (let's call that their love for God in their heart). For John Wesley, this parable is all about "faith working by love." For him, this parable is all about living out a life of holiness and faithfulness, even up until the very last hour.

Now, speaking of the last hour, some contemporary scholars argue that Paul was expecting the Lord to return in his lifetime. Some even said that he was wrong, that he was mistaken about the Lord's return. But if you look closely at His writings you will find, I think, evidence to the contrary. For example, in 1 Thessalonians we hear him encouraging the believers to work diligently for the Lord, during those last days: *Love one another more and more, aspire to live quietly, mind your own affairs, and to work with your hands, as we have directed you, so that you may behave properly toward outsiders and be dependent on no one.*[97] In Paul's understanding, this waiting was to be an active waiting. And we are still to be actively waiting for the Lord's return, and we still understand that it could be at anytime. But, of course, it is not for us to know the day or the hour.

Even so, we do need to be asking: How does a person actively wait? How can we be wise Christians with plenty of "love" to go along with our "faith"? How can we be ready for the Lord's return? Well, "faith working by love," as Wesley would say can only be attributed to God's active presence in our lives. You see, it's a "God Thing." But at the same time it's a "person thing" too. We are also "responsible." God gives us the ability to respond, but at the same time we have to be willing to follow through responsibly. Will my focus be on the things of this world, on daily worries and desires? Or will my focus be on the Bridegroom who will come?

That was the focus, the wisdom of the five bridesmaids that day who had enough "oil" for their "lamps." They chose to focus on the Bridegroom. And they were prepared. They had brought plenty of "love" to go along with their "faith." They had plenty of "love" because their lives had been focused on the Giver of that "love," all along. They had a close relationship with Him.

You know, the joy Jesus experienced as He walked this earth, came from doing what the Father sent Him to do. And He says to us: *"As the Father has sent Me, so I send you."*[98] We each have a niche in life, and spiritually, we find that niche when we are willing to spend our life serving the Lord.

"Do you love Me," Jesus asked Peter. *"Then feed My Sheep,"* He said.[99] Those who love the Lord will go about faithfully serving Him especially, in these last days. We don't know the day or the hour of His return. But we do know that that day and hour will come. And we do want to be among those who hear our Lord say: *"Well done, good and faithful servant."*[100]

John Wesley was once asked what he would do if he knew his Lord would return at the same time the next day. And he calmly replied: I would go to sleep, wake up in the morning, and go on with my work, for I would want the Lord to find me doing that which he had appointed me to do. Wesley was a man who was constantly about God's work, he was constantly burning that "oil of God's Love" in his "lamp of faith" and so he was able to say: "I am ready for the Lord's return."

Five bridesmaids went joyfully into the wedding banquet. Their "lamps of faith" were filled with the "oil of God's Love." They, like John Wesley, had "faith working by love." They were prepared. And those, our Lord called "wise." Amen.

Can a Rich Person Go to Heaven?

<u>Mark 10:17-25</u>
As he was setting out on a journey, a man ran up and knelt before him, and asked him, "Good Teacher, what must I do to inherit eternal life?" Jesus said to him, "Why do you call me good? No one is good but God alone. You know the commandments: 'You shall not murder; You shall not commit adultery; You shall not steal; You shall not bear false witness; You shall not defraud; Honor your father and mother.'" He said to him, "Teacher, I have kept all these since my youth." Jesus, looking at him, loved him and said, "You lack one thing; go, sell what you own, and give the money to the poor, and you will have treasure in heaven; then come, follow me." When he heard this, he was shocked and went away grieving, for he had many possessions. Then Jesus looked around and said to his disciples, "How hard it will be for those who have wealth to enter the kingdom of God!" And the disciples were perplexed at these words. But Jesus said to them again, "Children, how hard it is to enter the kingdom of God! It is easier for a camel to go through the eye of a needle than for someone who is rich to enter the kingdom of God."

A man named Murray once put the following announcement in his local church newsletter: "LOST: a black leather wallet containing precious family photos, personal ID documents, and $875. Finder can keep the photos and documents but please return the money, to which I am attached for sentimental reasons."

Another man replaced all the windows in his house with expensive double-pane energy efficient windows. A year later he got a call from the contractor complaining that his work had been completed a whole year and he had yet to pay for them. So, the man proceeded to tell the contractor just what his fast-talking salesman had told him last year, that in one year the windows would pay for themselves. So, why's the contractor complaining now?

A third-grade teacher asked her class to solve a math problem: "Suppose you had $.99 and your friend had $99. What would be the difference?" And one little girl replied, "The decimal point."

As Jesus started on his way, a man ran up to him and fell on his knees before him. "Good teacher," he asked, "what must I do to inherit eternal life?" *"Why do you call Me good?"* Jesus asked. *"No one is good -- except God alone. You know the commandments: 'Do not murder, do not commit adultery, do not steal, do not give false testimony, do not defraud, honor your father and mother.'"* "Teacher," he declared, "all these I have kept since I was a boy." *Jesus looked at him and loved him. "One thing you lack,"* He said. *"Go, sell everything you have and give to the poor, and you will have treasure in heaven. Then come, follow Me."* At this the man's face fell. He went away sad, because he had great wealth. Jesus looked around and said to His disciples: *"How hard it is for the rich to enter the kingdom of God!"* And the disciples were amazed at His words. Then Jesus said again: *"How hard it is to enter the kingdom of God! It is easier for a camel to go through the eye of a needle than for a rich man to enter the kingdom of God."* Wow, out of all of these stories concerning money, Jesus' teaching is the tough one, especially for a generation like ours that many times has to rent out mini-warehouses in order to store all its stuff. But there it is. *"It is easier for a camel to go through the eye of a needle than for a rich man to enter the kingdom of God."*

You know what? Money is a big deal in our lives. Let's just put it out on the table. We like nice things. We like things that are new, we like things that work. If they don't work, we just go and buy another one that does. It's pretty simple. How many of you guys have been longing for a new flat-screen TV? And, how many of you ladies wouldn't like to replace that slightly-worn living room furniture with something much more attractive? We like nice things, and in order to have nice things we've got to have the money. But Jesus warns us that money can ensnare us and separate us from God, if we are not careful. It's not the money itself that is bad; it's the separation from God that is bad for us.

Dr. Harry Emerson Fosdick once said: Our grandparents were reared to say: "What shall I do to be saved?" But this generation has been reared to say: "What shall I do to succeed?" That's our culture. And the scary thing is that it is difficult to cut ourselves loose from our culture.

There was once a story about an old monk who was mentoring a young disciple: Believing that he had the ability to be on his own, the monk allowed the boy to live in a lean-to near the river bank by himself. And at first, each night, happy as a lark, the young disciple put out his clothing, his only possession, to dry. One morning, though, he was dismayed to find that his clothing had been torn to shreds by rats. So he begged for a more clothing from the villagers. And when the rats came to destroy that set of clothing, he got a cat to keep the rats away. But then he had to beg, not only, for food for himself, but also for milk for the cat. So, to get around that, he bought a cow. But then he had to seek food for the cow. And finally, he concluded that it would be easier to work the land around his hut instead of begging. So during the time he would normally spend in prayer, he began to grow crops to feed the cow and himself. And when the operation expanded, well, he hired workers and he also married a woman who kept the house running smoothly. Pretty soon he was one of the wealthiest people in the village.

Several years later the monk came back to find a mansion where the lean-to had been. "What is the meaning of this?" the monk asked. And the disciple replied, "Father, there was no other way for me to keep the clothes I had on my back."[101] That's how it happens. Stuff becomes more important to us than our focus on God. Or as one comedian (George Carlin) said: Stuff is important. You gotta take care of your stuff. You gotta have a place for your stuff. Everybody's gotta have a place for their stuff. That's what life is all about: trying to find a place for your stuff. That's all your house is: a place to keep your stuff. If you didn't have so much stuff, you wouldn't need a house. You could just walk around all the time.

I wonder how many of us have ever felt oppressed by all our stuff? Where can we store it when we don't need it? How can we find it when we do need it? What do we do with all the clutter? And, most importantly, could it be that stuff is crowding out the spiritual dimension of our lives?

In the Hebrew tradition, wealthy people were the ones who could spend time reading the scriptures and praying. You can see that in the movie, Fiddler on the Roof, when a Jewish father sings: If I were a rich man, I'd have the time that I lack, to sit in the synagogue and pray. And maybe have a seat by the eastern wall, and I'd discuss the learned books with the holy men, seven hours every day, and that would be the sweetest thing of all. But that's not what's happening with us in this country. The more stuff we have, the less time, it seems, we have for God. We know that. But how can we disentangle ourselves from the social pressures, as well as, the inner greed that causes us to fill our lives with material things? And, what is the Christian's responsibility when it comes to wealth?

First of all, I think, we need to take control of our finances, so we can have more time to focus on God and His will for our lives. And second, we need to take control of our desires. Now, this one is a little more challenging.

But you can start by asking yourself, what would really improve the quality of my life? Often the things that will improve the quality of our lives don't really require a great outlay of money.

A few years ago, a book came out titled Trading Up. This book traced the roots of some of our misconceptions about wealth. The 1950s was a time of increasing prosperity in the United States. But even as personal wealth grew, spending habits changed little. The primary reason why Americans didn't become instant shopaholics, according to these authors, was guilt. What we had in the "50's was a generation that had been raised on hard work, thrift, and personal sacrifice. Well, the marketers realized that wealth would be accumulating in American pockets, and so, in response they began to change their advertising tactics. "In the 1960s they began to bombard the American public with a message that said: It is important for Americans to reach for their dreams, fulfill their emotional needs, be all they can be, grab for the gusto, self-actualize, and, not only do all that, but also take care of themselves, look after number one, reward themselves, and build their self-esteem." In other words, advertisers told Americans that the good life consisted of possessions that they accumulated. Advertisers tried to instill within American hearts, a "whoever dies with the most toys wins," mentality. And many bought into this concept.[102] So, today we have to ask: How do we escape this mentality?

One way might be to think about the really good times in your life. And then ask yourself: Was money really necessary for my enjoyment? For example, most of us need to exercise more. Well how about, rather than spending a lot of money on expensive exercise equipment, you resolve to take a walk each evening with your spouse? The time spent together can be a lot of fun, and you can also avoid being a couch potato, sitting in front of that new flat-screen TV, upon that attractive new sofa all evening long.

Or, maybe if you enjoy being around other people, you might want to get involved in a church project or a newly forming Discipleship Group, or possibly you might want to start up something else new, where people can gather to make a difference for the Lord. The method of escaping this mentality will differ for each of us, but we don't have to move in lock-step with the world around us, that's the thing. We can be different. In fact, as Christians, we are called to be different. If we set our minds to it, we can find alternatives to a lifestyle that requires the constant accumulation of un-necessary stuff.

Finally, and most importantly, remember that in our finances as well as everything else, God comes first. If anything in life comes before God, then we are not following Jesus Christ. If we can buy season football tickets, but cannot tithe, we have a spiritual problem. If we can make a payment on a nicer home, but cannot meet our responsibilities to God's church, we are worshiping mammon and not God. That's tough talk, I know, but as your pastor that's my job, to tell it like it is.

In one of his stories, Garrison Keillor tells about a Sunday morning in Lake Wobegon Lutheran Church. Here's the setting, it seemed that the sermon had gone on far too long, and Clarence Bunsen had checked out early. But then, he realized that it was almost time for the offering, so he quietly reached for his wallet. Upon opening his wallet, Clarence discovered that he had no cash. So, he took out his pen and hid the checkbook in the middle of his Bible, next to one of the Psalms. He began to scratch out a check for thirty dollars, because you see, he almost had a heart attack last week, and because somebody in the church would be counting the offering and he wanted them to know he gave his thirty dollars. He tried not to be obvious, but a lady to his right saw him. Clarence could tell that she thought he was writing in the pew Bible, so he didn't look to closely at what he was doing. Then when the offering plate came by, Clarence proudly put in the check, only to realize a moment too late that he had just written a check for three hundred dollars, instead of thirty as he intended.

But, what could he do? On the one hand, he could go downstairs after church and find the ushers counting the collection and say, "Hey, there's been a mistake. I gave more than I really wanted to." Or, he and his family could just eat beans and oatmeal for the rest of the month. Clarence thought quite some time about the situation, and then decided to trust that God was in control of it all, that his family would somehow get by, and that the contribution would be put to good use in the lives of others. And then an amazing thing happened. In that moment, Clarence felt fully alive for the first time in a long time.[103] And no wonder. Even though it was unintentional, for the first time in a long time, Clarence had put God first.

You know, giving is a spiritual discipline. And anytime we submit ourselves to a spiritual discipline, we will be blessed. These days, especially these days, we need to remember where abundant living really lies. And it's not with those things that take up space in our overcrowded houses or closets. It's not with those things that will be long forgotten someday, but it is with those things that will be eternal.

So what are we saying here? Well, when you take charge of your finances, and when you take charge of your desires, and when you put God and Jesus Christ first in your life, instead of going away sad like the rich young man, you will find out what it is to enter the Kingdom of God.

And finally, let me leave you with these words of our Lord. Jesus said: *"Give, and it will be given to you. A good measure, pressed down, shaken together, running over, will be put into your lap; for the measure you give will be the measure you get back."*[104] So be it. Amen.

Interruptions vs. Opportunities

<u>Mark 5:21-43</u>

When Jesus had crossed again in the boat to the other side, a great crowd gathered around him; and he was by the sea. Then one of the leaders of the synagogue named Jairus came and, when he saw him, fell at his feet and begged him repeatedly, "My little daughter is at the point of death. Come and lay your hands on her, so that she may be made well, and live." So he went with him. And a large crowd followed him and pressed in on him. Now there was a woman who had been suffering from hemorrhages for twelve years. She had endured much under many physicians, and had spent all that she had; and she was no better, but rather grew worse. She had heard about Jesus, and came up behind him in the crowd and touched his cloak, for she said, "If I but touch his clothes, I will be made well." Immediately her hemorrhage stopped; and she felt in her body that she was healed of her disease. Immediately aware that power had gone forth from him, Jesus turned about in the crowd and said, "Who touched my clothes?" And his disciples said to him, "You see the crowd pressing in on you; how can you say, 'Who touched me?'" He looked all around to see who had done it. But the woman, knowing what had happened to her, came in fear and trembling, fell down before him, and told him the whole truth. He said to her, "Daughter, your faith has made you well; go in peace, and be healed of your disease." While he was still speaking, some people came from the leader's house to say, "Your daughter is dead. Why trouble the teacher any further?" But overhearing what they said, Jesus said to the leader of the synagogue, "Do not fear, only believe." He allowed no one to follow him except Peter, James, and John, the brother of James. When they came to the house of the leader of the synagogue, he saw a commotion, people weeping and wailing loudly. When he had entered, he said to them, "Why do you make a commotion and weep? The child is not dead but sleeping." And they laughed at him. Then he put them all outside, and took the child's father and mother and those who were with him, and went in where the child was.

He took her by the hand and said to her, "Talitha cum," which means, "Little girl, get up!" And immediately the girl got up and began to walk about (she was twelve years of age). At this they were overcome with amazement. He strictly ordered them that no one should know this, and told them to give her something to eat.

We all know the importance of time and how valuable it is. But no matter what we do, time continues to slip away, one second after another. It waits for no one. Even so, busyness does not always equal blessedness. It's how we invest our time that makes the difference. The shortness of time in this life is not a new problem. For example, people, for years, have been talking about the fact that life, itself is so short. And the fact of the matter is, that even in 2008, we have not figured out how to slow time down or how to get more than 24 hours into our day. And just as it was a thousand years ago, we only get one chance to use each second wisely. We don't get a second chance. We don't get any do-overs. When it's gone, it's gone. And so we ask: What can we do? Well, hopefully, we can try to invest our time in a way that is pleasing to God.

You know, it has been said that the time between Thanksgiving and New Years Day is the busiest time of the year. So what better time, then the Sunday before Thanksgiving, to talk about how we can invest such a great commodity wisely?

Let us pray: May the words of my mouth and the meditations of each of our hearts be acceptable in Your sight, O God, our Rock and our Redeemer. Amen.

Concerning life and time a poet once wrote: When I was a child I laughed and wept and time crept. When I was a youth I dreamed and talked and time walked. But, when I became full grown, time ran. And even later as older I grew, time flew. Soon I shall find while traveling on that time is gone.

We only have a certain amount of time here on this earth and we don't ever seem to have enough of it. Even though we live in an age of fiber optics and laser speeds, time still manages to fly by much more quickly than we would like. People advise us to utilize every second of our day wisely. And many are making millions teaching us how to manage our time. Yet, I think, that in our trying to cram so much into every 24-hour period, we are missing much of life's meaning. In this age of organization and time management, something has gotten lost. Yes, we are doing more in a shorter span of time, but are we really experiencing a greater quality of life? Or are we missing out on many God given opportunities because we are too busy?

Today's question is this: How will you deal with things that interrupt your daily schedule, you know, like the telephone call that breaks your concentration or takes you from your computer or your favorite football game or television show? What about the chance encounter with an old friend at the Post Office or grocery store? Do you consider that telephone call or chance meeting or anything else for that matter, as an undesirable interruption?

Time, even if we go all the way back to the first century, time is short. Let's do that, let's go back to the time of Jesus and take a look at what He did with His daily schedule. He had only a little while, three years, to do the work that His Father had sent Him to do. He knew that He needed to make each moment count because time would quickly slip away. So how did He plan His day? Did He have a busy organized schedule that couldn't allow for interruptions?

Well, Mark gives us a glimpse of what a day in the life of Jesus looked like. He writes: *When Jesus returned to Capernaum after some days, it was reported that He was at home. So many gathered around that there was no longer room for them, not even in front of the door; and He was speaking the word to them. Then some people came, bringing to Him a paralyzed man, carried by four of them. And when they could not bring him to Jesus because of the crowd, they removed the roof above Him; and after having dug through it, they let down the mat on which the paralytic lay. When Jesus saw their faith, He said to the paralytic, "Son, your sins are forgiven." And so that those present would know that the Son of Man had authority on earth to forgive sins-- He said to the paralytic – stand up, take your mat and go to your home." And he stood up, and immediately took the mat and went out before all of them; so that they were all amazed and glorified God, saying, "We have never seen anything like this!"*[105]

Now, this story was so important that it was recorded in three of the four Gospel accounts. And it is in Luke's account that we hear that Jesus was speaking to the Pharisees and some of the teachers of the law. You see, they had come from Galilee, Judea and Jerusalem. But, as Jesus was addressing this audience of religious people, some other people lowered a crippled man through a hole they had made in the roof. He was lowered down and rested right at the feet of Jesus. Now, talk about an interruption. Jesus was probably making a very important point in His teaching when all of a sudden this man is lowered right in front of Him. Jesus could have rebuked the people who lowered the paralytic from the roof. He could have become angry for being interrupted in the middle of His teaching. He could have been upset about the mess they had made of the ceiling, but He wasn't. No, instead Jesus saw that the friends of this handicapped man thought so much about him that they made a courageous effort to present the man for healing. Sure this was an interruption. Sure it happened in the middle of an important teachable moment. But Jesus saw the interruption as a means to glorify His Father in heaven.

And then later on in Mark's Gospel, Jesus was returning to Galilee from the region of the Gerasenes. He had come to address another large crowd that had gathered there. But before He could begin His speech a ruler of the synagogue came and fell at His feet pleading with him to come to his house because his only daughter was dying. Jesus could have told the man: Hey, can't you see that a very large crowd has gathered to hear Me speak? Don't you realize that this is an important meeting? Don't you realize that I only have a three-year ministry on this earth? But Jesus didn't rebuke the man. He followed the man to his house. As He followed the man, the crowds pressed close to see Him. Mark says that the crowds almost crushed Him. And in that crowd was a woman who had spent all that she had on doctors. They had been unable to cure her. She pushed through the crowd and grabbed the hem of Jesus' robe and immediately she was healed. When Jesus felt the tug on His robe He turned and asked: *"Who touched Me?"*

Another interruption, picture it, Jesus has returned to Galilee to speak to the large crowd that has gathered. He is interrupted by a man who wants Him to come to his house and heal his daughter. Then, as He is going to deal with that interruption, He is interrupted again, this time by a woman who grabs His robe. Each day of His ministry went that way. Once, lepers who wanted to be healed encountered Him. Another time a centurion stopped Him to ask that his daughter be healed. Yet, another time some little children came and wanted to sit on His lap during a teaching lesson – one interruption after another. How could Jesus cope with all of this? God had sent Him to earth to accomplish a mission. He only had a short time to do what His Father had instructed Him to do. He began each day with a game plan. He had a schedule but it got interrupted each and every day. Was Jesus a poor manager of time? And if not, why did He allow all of these interruptions? Well, the answer is simple: Jesus saw the interruptions as opportunities to bring glory to God.

Now, let's look at your life and my life for a moment. Each day we begin with a game plan, right? That is, we have a schedule or a plan for the day. For you it may mean going to work five days a week and then planning the evenings and the weekends with chores and/or some kind of entertainment or worship. Or if you've reached that golden age, well, from what I have been told, you are even busier now than you were before you retired. But, how do you react when a special church program or event clashes with something else you had planned? Or, how do you react when you have your Saturday all mapped out and a friend needs you to come over and help them? Or, how do you react when your spouse or your child or your grandchild needs time with you and your schedule is, oh, so busy? Or, outside your circle of family and friends, how do you respond to interruptions at the post office, the grocery store or Wal-Mart. Do you see them as opportunities to witness for Christ? Or, when you see a person who obviously needs help, are you in too big of a hurry to offer help? In other words: Is you life too busy to serve God?

Each day our game plan will have interruptions. And we can respond, basically, in one of two ways. We can be irritated and curtly dismiss them as impasses and detours, or we can use them as opportunities to help others, and to glorify God.

Concerning what is truly important, a woman named Mable once said: It is more important to know where you are going than to get there quickly.[106] Jesus would have agreed with Mabel, I think. Jesus realized the importance of seizing the moment, even if it meant that His agenda for the day would have to change. There were times when He healed people that weren't on His appointment list, many times when His disciples needed teaching alone with Him, and many times when He needed to be alone in prayer with the Father, instead of being out there physically doing something in the community. We Christians need to think about how Jesus lived out His days and we need to learn from the way He invested His time. You know, some of the most important opportunities that we will ever have to glorify God, strangely enough, will be interruptions.

Let me leave you with these thoughts. How often have you talked with someone on the telephone who seemed to be in a hurry and wanted to get on with more important business? Or how often have you visited with someone in person, and received that same hurried feeling? You've probably experienced it, and didn't enjoy it. Or, perhaps, you were the one guilty of placing your agenda ahead of an interruption.

If you have ever done that, why not decide to tithe some of your time? Save up chunks, bits and pieces of time, and give it away to people who interrupt your pre-established plans. It is a great principle of love, to think of unexpected encounters as a good thing. Perhaps there shouldn't even be such a word as interruption, because when people come and alter your busy schedule even if for a brief moment, that encounter can be a wonderful moment for the both of you. Relish it. Probe it. Invest some of the time you have already decided to tithe. You know, we can't afford to indulge in the luxury of thinking that we are "too busy or to important."

Think about it, we have time for such inanimate things as pieces of mail, vast shopping trips or a television program beginning at 7:30. But what about our relationships with other people, isn't that a great deal of what life is all about anyway, being with and loving other people?

Remember Jesus? He didn't race about, hurrying from one city to another, collecting great crowds on the way just to give them a few moments of hurried heaven-data, so that He could dash off to the next place. No, instead, He invested time in people. In a crowd, a woman touched His robe. Lots of people were pushing against Him, touching His robe, but He discerned the urgency in this particular touch. He stopped, and He tithed a part of His time.

His disciples were full of fire and computer-like- efficiency. They wanted to get on with the task of getting something done, even if they really didn't understand what that "something" was. Jesus said, no, we have interruptions to tend to. Once a group of children came along and wanted to climb on His lap. And He said, let them stay. Let's enjoy them and let them enjoy us.[107] This Man from heaven knew and expressed the great worth of all individuals no matter who they were. He always patiently worked with the interruptions of His day.

Likewise, the apostle Paul prayed: *May God, who gives patience, steadiness, and encouragement, help you to live in complete harmony with each other – each with the attitude of Christ toward the other.*[108] The next time a person "interrupts" you, think not of your work and your deadlines; but, rather, think of that person's needs and of their hidden compliment in desiring to spend a few moments with you. Your meeting may be much more significant than you could ever imagine. Because, after all, it is an encounter with another person who is created in God's image. You may impart something crucial to their fulfillment – or they to yours.

The psalmist wrote: *"Teach us to number our days aright, that we may gain a heart of wisdom."*[109] May God grant us wisdom to use our time during this busiest season of the year wisely, seeing interruptions, not as such, but instead as wonderful God given opportunities to serve and to witness for Christ. Amen.

Turkey Day, and More

You know, no one celebrates Thanksgiving quite the way we do in this country, and for good reason, I think. You see, few people on earth have as much for which to be thankful as we do.

Nightline host Ted Koppel immigrated to the United States from England in his early teen years. The Koppels were originally from Germany, but had moved to England at the start of World War II. They had lived through food rationing, and had known the scarcity and desperation that accompanies war.

So a few years later, when young Ted heard a jingle in America on the radio about an antacid that could heal the pain of overeating, he began to cry. You see, he couldn't imagine that he now lived in a country where people could actually be able to eat too much.[110] We have so much in this country. And really, newcomers are more conscious of our blessings than many of us are.

The Reverend Enrico Sartorio had worked with lots of Italian immigrants in his ministry, and sometimes he helped with the translation of phrases from English to Italian. One day, after a lengthy discussion about Thanksgiving with a new Italian immigrant, the immigrant announced to the audience before them: Americans celebrate "Tacchins-giving Day" "tacchin" is their word for turkey "and that," he said, "is a very special day in America where people go door-to-door, giving away turkeys."[111] Well, he was part-right, many people and numerous churches and agencies do, give away turkeys for Thanksgiving Day. But really, Thanksgiving is much, much more than a national holiday set aside just to celebrate the eating of a big bird. For most of us, of course, our Thanksgiving holiday lasts longer than one day; theoretically, it can last as long as there are still leftovers in the fridge.

Michael Morse once made this memorable pun, saying: "If someone is addicted to eating Thanksgiving leftovers, can they quit cold turkey?"[112] Now, I have nothing against turkey, and all the good stuff that goes along with it, but I don't think it should be our central focus on Thanksgiving Day.

And contrary to all the sales flyers that will be stuffed into our mail boxes, Thanksgiving is not about shopping either. Did you know that over the next few weeks, advertisers will spend billions of dollars trying to convince us that our holidays won't be complete unless we buy their product, be it applesauce, power tools or a big screen TV?

It is amazing when we contemplate how much money, resources and effort will be invested in making us feel discontent with what we already have or don't have. And, we can easily become cynical about the holidays if we focus too much on the commercial aspect of it.

Thanksgiving is about, much more than eating turkey, watching football, or getting a head start on our Christmas shopping. The apostle Paul knew about Thanksgiving even though he didn't live in a culture that celebrated it as we do. Paul was continually giving thanks. He had a gratitude attitude. But, Paul didn't believe that gratitude was a solitary attribute for the believer. Gratitude, for him, was to be linked to caring for others. If God has blessed us, he would say, then we should seek to be a blessing for others.

Our lesson this evening comes from an Epistle that Paul wrote to the believers in Corinth, where he asked them to take up a collection to give to their poor brothers and sisters in Macedonia. He knew that the Corinthians wanted to hang on to their money just as much as we do today. So in order to "sell" his plan, he reminded them of the blessings God had poured out on them, saying: *The one who sows sparingly will also reap sparingly, and the one who sows bountifully will also reap bountifully. Each of you must give as you have made up your mind, not reluctantly or under compulsion, for God loves a cheerful giver. And God is able to provide you with every blessing in abundance, so that by always having enough of everything, you may share abundantly in every good work. As it is written, He scatters abroad, He gives to the poor; His righteousness endures forever; He who supplies seed to the sower and bread for food will supply and multiply your seed for sowing and increase the harvest of your righteousness. You will be enriched in every way for your great generosity, which will produce thanksgiving to God through us; for the rendering of this ministry not only supplies the needs of the saints but also overflows with many thanksgivings to God. Through the testing of this ministry you glorify God by your obedience to the confession of the gospel of Christ and by the generosity of your sharing with them and with all others, while they long for you and pray for you because of the surpassing grace of God that He has given you. Thanks be to God for His indescribable gift!*[113] This is quite a remarkable passage. What it says is that thankfulness and generosity feed on each other.

Find a person who is truly thankful and you will find a person who is generous. Find a person who is generous and you will find a person who is truly thankful. You see, thanksgiving is a constantly renewable resource. Thanksgiving produces generosity. And generosity brings a sense of abundance into our lives, which increases our thankfulness.

But, you know, we're used to thinking in terms of scarcity instead, aren't we? There's never enough to go around, we think. News reports warn us that if we don't exercise careful stewardship of our natural resources, we're going to run out of clean water, food, oil, land, and many other things. Many of us are haunted by the fear that we are just a few paychecks away from falling through the cracks. Therefore, we are more conscious of our scarcity than we are of our abundance. There's never enough time to get everything done, never enough money to make us feel truly secure, never enough love for us to get our fill. You've got to hold on to what you have, right? But because the season of Thanksgiving is a time to celebrate our abundance, the spirit of this season actually creates in us an abundance mind-set. When we focus on the positives in our life, we feel thankful. The more thankful we feel, the more joyful we feel. And joy is contagious. It overflows, and we want to share more with others. And we're never too young to put this lesson into practice.

Just ask Linda Moore, the mother of two young boys. The refrigerator in the Moore household has pictures on it of a cow and two goats. Not so unusual, perhaps. Most of us have odd stuff on our refrigerator door. What is unusual about the Moore household is that the cow's name is Camera Phone. The goats are named Sega Genesis I and Sega Genesis II. Some of you younger folks will probably recognize the latter two names as popular video games. One night, Linda Moore was watching TV with her two young boys when they saw an ad for an overseas charity for children. According to the ad, twenty dollars would feed one child for a month. Moore mentioned to her sons that they had planned on spending twenty dollars per month on a faster Internet service. Then she asked them to decide where the money should go. Well, they voted unanimously for the children's charity. After that, Moore found new ways to help her boys develop the spirit of giving.

Each time they wanted to make a purchase, she asked them to weigh it against sending money to charity. She obtained a catalogue from a charity that gives farm animals to people in poverty stricken areas. The animals can be used for meat, milk, eggs, leather. And the boys responded generously. So, instead of a camera phone, they had a picture of a cow on their refrigerator, and instead of video games, they had pictures of goats. Did the boys resent this emphasis on helping others? If so, they didn't let it show. In fact, the boys were so excited by this opportunity that they began picking up odd jobs around the neighborhood in order to raise money to give more.[114] This story proves a second principle that enriches our lives: Thanksgiving reaches its highest point when we share our blessings with others.

Now, we talked about how joy is so contagious that it has to be passed on to others. And when we do that, thankfulness and joy is created in other people. And when those people praise God for our obedience, and pray God's blessings upon us, He blesses us in response to their prayers. And the thankfulness and joy start all over again. This is what Paul was trying to explain to the believers in Corinth.

When Amanda was just a little child, she dreamed of owning a brand-new purple bicycle. She worked at odd jobs and saved up every penny in order to buy herself the perfect purple bicycle. And every night she prayed for that purple bicycle. But one day, Amanda's Sunday school teacher told the class about a missionary's son in Chile who had contracted hepatitis. The teacher wanted the class to buy the boy something to cheer him up. The children voted to buy the missionary's son a bicycle. Amanda's little heart broke at the thought of giving up her money, but she knew that the missionary's son needed it more than she did. So she gave every hard-earned dollar to the Sunday school teacher.

Years later, Amanda fell in love with a college classmate named Phillip. Amanda's and Phillip's families came together for a big dinner to celebrate their children's engagement. At the family dinner, Phillip's parents shared stories from their years serving as missionaries overseas. One of their hardest times, they recalled, was when the whole family fell ill while serving in Chile. Phillip had contracted hepatitis, and he was the sickest of them all. What joy he experienced when he received a brand-new bicycle from the generous kids back in the United States! Amanda cried as she realized that the sacrifice of her bicycle money had gone to bless the life of her future husband.[115] Now, God does work in mysterious ways, doesn't He? Who knows what effect your giving will have on the lives of others?

Generosity and thankfulness feed on one another. Give generously and your sense of thankfulness will grow. And the more thankful you are, the more generous you will want to be. It's an important and time-tested principle of Christian living. No wonder Paul wrote: *"Thank God for these twin gifts of generosity and thankfulness. No language can praise them enough!"* And so, my challenge for us this evening is for each one of us to focus more fully on jump starting the thankfulness cycle in our lives, by looking for more ways in which we can bless others with our generosity. Now, that's the spirit of Thanksgiving. Amen.

Comfort, Needed

Isaiah 40:1-11

Comfort, O comfort my people, says your God. Speak tenderly to Jerusalem, and cry to her that she has served her term, that her penalty is paid, that she has received from the Lord's hand double for all her sins. A voice cries out: "In the wilderness prepare the way of the LORD, make straight in the desert a highway for our God. Every valley shall be lifted up, and every mountain and hill be made low; the uneven ground shall become level, and the rough places a plain. Then the glory of the LORD shall be revealed, and all people shall see it together, for the mouth of the LORD has spoken." A voice says, "Cry out!" And I said, "What shall I cry?" All people are grass, their constancy is like the flower of the field. The grass withers, the flower fades, when the breath of the LORD blows upon it; surely the people are grass. The grass withers, the flower fades; but the word of our God will stand forever. Get you up to a high mountain, O Zion, herald of good tidings; lift up your voice with strength, O Jerusalem, herald of good tidings, lift it up, do not fear; say to the cities of Judah, "Here is your God!" See, the Lord GOD comes with might, and his arm rules for him; his reward is with him, and his recompense before him. He will feed his flock like a shepherd; he will gather the lambs in his arms, and carry them in his bosom, and gently lead the mother sheep.

Just for the fun of it, we are going to begin each of our next three Advent messages by recalling a Christmas song. Some of the songs will be secular and some will be sacred. Our song for today is several decades old. It was first sung by a young rock-and-roller named Elvis Presley. I'm sure you remember him and you will probably remember the song too: "I'll have a blue, blue, Christmas without you."

"Blue Christmas," I thought this song would be appropriate because our reading begins with the prophet Isaiah saying: *"Comfort, O comfort my people, says your God."* Comfort, that's our theme for this second Sunday in Advent. Because, you know, not everyone is full of cheer at Christmas. In fact, this is the season when depression is at a peak for some people.

Now, there was another song I considered for today, it's called: "Please Daddy (Don't Get Drunk This Christmas)." That one didn't reach the popularity of "Blue Christmas," though. Can you guess who first sang this Christmas classic? Well, it was the late, great folk singer, John Denver. Clean-cut and wholesome, "Rocky Mountain High," John Denver, singing from the point of view of a little eight-year-old child, Denver reminisces about a Christmas when Daddy drank too much and fell down underneath the Christmas tree, much to Mommy's dismay. And he asks Daddy to show some restraint this year because he doesn't "want to see Mommy cry" anymore. Denver didn't sell many records with this tune, but for some people this sentimental song will be all-too-relevant during this time of year. And it too, reminds us that holiday memories aren't necessarily happy in all families.[116]

Let us pray: May the words of my mouth and the meditations of each of our hearts be acceptable in Your sight, O God, our Rock and our Redeemer. Amen.

"Comfort, O comfort my people, says your God," writes the prophet Isaiah. *Comfort, O comfort my people, says your God. Speak tenderly to Jerusalem, and cry to her that she has served her term, that her penalty is paid, that she has received from the Lord's hand double for all her sins. A voice cries out: "In the wilderness prepare the way of the LORD, make straight in the desert a highway for our God. Every valley shall be lifted up, and every mountain and hill be made low; the uneven ground shall become level, and the rough places a plain. Then the glory of the LORD shall be revealed, and all people shall see it together, for the mouth of the LORD has spoken."*[117]

Now, if you can identify in any form or fashion with something less than joy when everyone else seems to be filled with joy, well, here is God's word for your life right now. If you are in pain this Advent season, God is here to comfort you. If you are in grief over the loss of a loved one, or perhaps this year was not the year financially you had hoped for. If the economy has you worried, or, if you have received a bad medical report for yourself or someone in your family. Or if your marriage is coming apart or if you're having to deal with other family problems, well, I want you to know that there is hope. There is hope because, whatever your heartbreak is this day, God wants to offer you His comfort.

Advent says, first of all, that God cares about a broken world. Isaiah was speaking to a broken nation. Much of the nation of Israel had been carried away into exile. They longed to return to their home land. And Isaiah assured them that God had not forgotten them nor forsaken them. Their suffering was almost over. God would build a vast highway over which they could travel through the wilderness from Babylon back to their home, back to the Promised Land. In the New Testament John the Baptist talks about an even more important highway linking humanity and God through the coming of Jesus Christ. The New and the Old Testament message is the same. God cares about a broken world. God cares about broken people.

Brian Abel Ragan's father used to tell him a folk tale (a fable) every Christmas when he was growing up. It was about a little boy who was very poor. His widowed mother struggled to make ends meet. The little boy had only one toy, a sad little car in awful condition. It had only one window and two wheels. The roof was smashed in. But the boy loved that car. It was almost Christmas and the boy knew there would be no presents. But he was excited anyway. It was the first year he would be allowed to go to midnight service on Christmas Eve.

He couldn't wait. He knew that, before the service began, people would bring gifts to the Christ child. He had been told the gifts were magnificent jeweled chalices for the altar, new clothes for poor children like himself, and envelopes full of money. The little boy wanted very much to give the Christ child a present. And so he set out to earn enough money before Christmas to do just that. On the afternoon of Christmas Eve, he sat at the kitchen table counting out what he had earned. He had enough money to buy a fine present for the Christ child. But before he could put the money back in his pocket his mother returned home. "Oh, son," she said, "What a good boy you are! Now we can have a real Christmas dinner!" And she scooped up the money and hurried off to get to the market before it closed. The little boy was heartbroken. What was he going to do now? Well, about that time he remembered his broken toy car. He knew it was the only thing he had to give the Christ child, so he put the car in his pocket and set off for church. When he arrived the pews were filling up. He walked timidly to the manger scene which was set up before one of the side altars. Magnificent gifts were already piled up before the Christ child. The little boy laid his broken toy car amid all the treasures. He squeezed into a pew close by just as the organ began playing the prelude. About this time one of the ushers took a last look at the manger scene to see if everything was in place. Suddenly he spied the car. "Who would leave a piece of trash like this at Our Lord's crib?" he said loudly enough for the boy to hear. The usher picked up the toy car and threw it aside. The little boy was crushed. There was no time for him to retrieve his gift. The organ was playing and the procession had begun. Then suddenly, everything came to a dead stop. To the amazement of all present, the baby in the manger came to life and crawled across the stone floor. He crawled until he reached the broken car. Then carefully he tucked it under his arm and crawled back to the manger. By this time all the people had fallen to their knees.

At this point the priest rose and approached the manger. There, just as before, was a plaster child with a halo, but now he smiled and his arms were folded tightly around a broken toy car. Brian Abel Ragan remembers hearing his father tell this folk tale and he resented it. You see, he didn't like his father. His father had problems with alcohol. The song "Please Daddy (Don't Get Drunk This Christmas)" could have been written for him. Ragan had a difficult time forgiving his father. He felt his father was trying to use this story to manipulate him into being a more obedient son. With time, however, Ragan came to put this little Christmas story into perspective. "As I think of my father's Christmas story now," says the grown-up Ragan, "I realize that I cast him in the wrong role. My father was not the good little boy who gave his last plaything to the Lord. No, my father was the smashed, car, He was a wreck. But despite or because of all this, he clearly longed to be cradled in his Savior's arms, to have Christ still seek him after he had been rejected by everyone else."[118]

Here's why we call the story of Jesus "Good News." God cares about a broken world. God cares about broken people. That's what Advent and Christmas are all about. *"Comfort, O comfort my people, says your God."*

Secondly, Jesus came into our world to identify with the world's suffering. Stephen Arterburn in his book *Flashpoints* tells about a remarkable young woman named Pattie Moore. When Pattie was seventeen years old, she was a promising student at the Rochester Institute of Technology in Rochester, New York. One day a bus she was riding on stopped for a traffic light at a busy intersection. An old man on the sidewalk caught Moore's attention. He was disheveled, but clean and he carried two loaded shopping bags, one under each arm. He moved slowly. Each step seemed to be a challenge for him. This was an awakening for Pattie Moore. It suddenly occurred to her that older people have special needs, special difficulties. This became a major motivator in her life.

After graduation Pattie moved to New York City and accepted a job with a prestigious industrial design firm where she began to design products with older people in mind. Then one day Pattie decided to go even further. With the help of a friend who was a makeup artist, Pattie decided to spend several months disguised as an old woman. She wanted to discover for herself how America treated the elderly. She reported that she was ignored, shoved, cheated, ostracized, and even mugged. "If I got a smile or a hello from a passerby, I felt like I'd received a hug from God himself," Pattie replied. Her experiment changed forever her thinking about the needs of the elderly. It also influenced the thinking of industrial designers, politicians, and others who learned about Pattie's work.[119] The only way Pattie Moore could learn about the needs of the elderly was to experience for herself what it was like to be elderly.

Here is what is so majestic about the coming of Christ. God came to us as a tiny baby. Other religions have gods that come to earth, but only the Christian faith speaks of a God who emptied Himself completely and went through the entire human experience. God knows the challenges we face. God knows the pain of being human. The highway that God constructed between heaven and earth was a two-way road. God came down to us so that we might go up to Him. God came into this world to walk in your shoes. God knows your pain. This is the Gospel. This is the Good News. God cares about a broken world. Jesus came into our world to identify with the world's suffering.

And finally the last point: The manger of Bethlehem is as much a part of Christian faith as the cross of Calvary. I love the way Isaiah puts it in verse nine: *You who bring good tidings to Zion, go up on a high mountain. You who bring good tidings to Jerusalem, lift up your voice with a shout, lift it up, do not be afraid; say to the towns of Judah, "Here is your God!"* Here is your God, a helpless baby in the manger of Bethlehem. Here is your God, baptized by John in the river Jordan. Here is your God, teaching and healing beside the Sea of Galilee. Here is your God, hanging on the cross of Calvary, making the ultimate sacrifice.

I don't know about shouting, like Isaiah prescribes, but maybe that would be appropriate, because Isaiah is telling us who God is, as he says: *He tends His flock like a shepherd: He gathers the lambs in His arms and carries them close to His heart; He gently leads those that have young.* Here is your God, the prophet says.

God cares about a broken world. Jesus came into the world to identify with our suffering. And the manger of Bethlehem is just as important to our faith as the cross of Calvary. And so, during this Advent season, don't forget to look in the manger of Bethlehem whatever your need may be, look into the manger of Bethlehem, because it is there that you will hear the words of the prophet echoing back to you: *"Here is your God."* Amen.

Let It Shine!

<u>John 1:6-14</u>
There was a man sent from God, whose name was John. He came as a witness to testify to the light, so that all might believe through him. He himself was not the light, but he came to testify to the light. The true light, which enlightens everyone, was coming into the world. He was in the world, and the world came into being through him; yet the world did not know him. He came to what was his own, and his own people did not accept him. But to all who received him, who believed in his name, he gave power to become children of God, who were born, not of blood or of the will of the flesh or of the will of man, but of God. And the Word became flesh and lived among us, and we have seen his glory, the glory as of a father's only son, full of grace and truth.

Our Advent song for today is: "This little light of mine, I'm gonna let it shine." You see, the writer of the Gospel of John refers to Christ as the light of the world. Light was coming into our world, he said. And even today, we believe that, and maybe that's why we adorn our Christmas trees with hundreds of lights.

John the Baptist was the voice of one calling in the desert, *"Make straight the way for the Lord. He came as a witness to testify concerning the light, so that through him all might believe. He himself was not the light; he came only as a witness to the light."* The light, of course, was Jesus. When John wrote his Gospel the world was in darkness. And so, he wanted the world to know that a light had penetrated that darkness.

Now, I think we all understand how important light is to life, especially if your electricity has gone out for any length of time. Charles Colson once told about a meeting he and several other Christian leaders had with the president of Ecuador, a man named Rodrigo Borja Cevallos. These Christian leaders were asking the president for permission to begin a ministry in Ecuadorian prisons. And at that, the president interrupted their conversation because he wanted to tell a story of his own imprisonment years before being elected to the presidency. Cevallos had been involved in the struggle for democracy in Ecuador. And when the military cracked down, Cevallos was arrested. Without trial, they threw him into a cold dungeon with no light and no window. For three days he endured total darkness and he feared for his sanity. Just when the situation seemed unbearable, though, the door to his cell opened, and someone crept into the darkness. The president heard this person working on something in the opposite corner. Then the figure crept out, closed the door, and disappeared. Minutes later the room suddenly blazed with light. Someone, at the risk perhaps of his own life, had connected electricity to the broken light fixture. "From that moment," explained Cevallos, "my imprisonment had meaning because at least I could see."[120]

Anyone who has ever found themselves in darkness for whatever reason knows what a welcome relief light is. Luci Swindoll tells about a friend who, along with six strangers, was caught in a stalled elevator during a power failure. Fear was quickly turning to panic. But then Luci's friend remembered that she had a tiny flashlight in her purse. When she turned it on, the fear in the elevator dissipated. For forty-five minutes these strangers sat around the light and talked, laughed, and even sang. That little light came on just when this group of strangers needed it the most.[121] Just when the world most needed God's light, a babe was born in Bethlehem. Jesus is the light that shined in the darkness and the darkness has not overcome it.

The light of Christ will never stop shining. Through wars, pestilence, famine, good times and bad, the light of Christ will continue to shine.

Our grandparents saw its glow in the darkest hours of the depression. Our soldiers saw its glow even on distant battlefields. The light shines in the darkness and the darkness has not overcome it. Senator McCain once wrote a story for *Reader's Digest.* It was about the time he spent as a prisoner of war in Vietnam. Any of you who know his story know he was cruelly mistreated in that prison camp. Fortunately, he and the other prisoners were given a little freedom as the time drew closer for them to go home. This increased freedom made for a very special Christmas. The prisoners were gathered in a dimly lit room with one light bulb. With solemn awareness of where they were and what they had been through, they began to sing "Silent Night" and exchange crude handmade gifts. John McCain remembers it as his best Christmas ever.

No matter where we find ourselves, the world cannot extinguish the light of Christ. That light shines in prison camps. It shines in hospital rooms and funeral parlors. It shines amidst poverty and every manner of heartache and hardship. Nothing can stop it. Neither life nor death nor powers nor principalities, nor anything in all of creation, can stop the light of Christ, the light of God's love for humanity, from penetrating the darkness. John declares that fact so beautifully when he writes: *In Him was life, and the life was the light of all people. The light shines in the darkness, and the darkness did not overcome it.*[122]

Now, even though the world may not yet fully understand, Jesus is still the light of the world, and that light can never be extinguished. But this is what I want you to remember, remember that the greatest privilege of all, is to be able to share that light with someone else. "This little light of mine, I'm gonna let it shine; this little light of mine, I'm gonna let it shine."

John was not the light. He came to bear witness to the light and that, my fellow Christians is our job as well. And what a great and wonderful privilege it is for us to be able to do that for our God. Do you understand that this is our call as followers of Jesus Christ, to shine His light into the life of anyone who is sitting in darkness? John was not the light, but he came to bear witness to the light. That light was Christ, who is the life and the light of the whole world. And now we have the same privilege that John the Baptist had.

"This little light of mine, (SING WITH ME); I'm gonna let it shine; this little light of mine, I'm gonna let it shine; this little light of mine, I'm gonna let it shine. Let it shine, let it shine, let it shine." That's our job when we leave this sanctuary today; our job is to let the light of Christ shine through us. Remember that. Amen.

Mary, Did You Know?

Luke 1:26-38
In the sixth month the angel Gabriel was sent by God to a town in Galilee called Nazareth, to a virgin engaged to a man whose name was Joseph, of the house of David. The virgin's name was Mary. And he came to her and said, "Greetings, favored one! The Lord is with you." But she was much perplexed by his words and pondered what sort of greeting this might be. The angel said to her, "Do not be afraid, Mary, for you have found favor with God. And now, you will conceive in your womb and bear a son, and you will name him Jesus. He will be great, and will be called the Son of the Most High, and the Lord God will give to him the throne of his ancestor David. He will reign over the house of Jacob forever, and of his kingdom there will be no end." Mary said to the angel, "How can this be, since I am a virgin?" The angel said to her, "The Holy Spirit will come upon you, and the power of the Most High will overshadow you; therefore the child to be born will be holy; he will be called Son of God. And now, your relative Elizabeth in her old age has also conceived a son; and this is the sixth month for her who was said to be barren. For nothing will be impossible with God." Then Mary said, "Here am I, the servant of the Lord; let it be with me according to your word." Then the angel departed from her.

One of the most beautiful of the modern Christmas songs was written by a man who is best known, perhaps, as a comedian. His name is Mark Lowry. Lowry is also a musician and he performed for many years with the Gaither Vocal band. In 1984 he was asked to write some words for his local church choir and he wrote a poem that began like this. "Mary, did you know that your baby boy would one day walk on water? Mary, did you know that your baby boy would save our sons and daughters?"

A few years later guitarist Buddy Greene added a perfectly matched tune and a wonderful song was born. "Mary did you know that your baby boy has walked where angels trod? And when you kiss your little baby, you kiss the face of God!" "Mary, did you know that your baby boy is Lord of all creation? Mary, did you know that your baby boy will one day rule the nations?"[123] The song's been around now for nearly two decades. The most popular version is sung by Kenny Rogers and Wynonna Judd. "Mary, did you know?"

Let us pray: May the words of my mouth and the meditations of each of our hearts be acceptable in Your sight, O God, our Rock and our Redeemer. Amen.

How could Mary know what was happening to her when the angel Gabriel showed up? Only Luke tells this story. He tells the story of Jesus' birth from Mary's point of view. The angel Gabriel is the messenger of God. He's already announced to Zechariah that his wife, Elizabeth (Mary's relative) would have a son too, despite her old age. Then Gabriel visits Mary. Luke begins the story by telling us that: *In the sixth month the angel Gabriel was sent by God to a town in Galilee called Nazareth, to a virgin engaged to a man whose name was Joseph, of the house of David. The virgin's name was Mary. And he came to her and said, "Greetings, favored one! The Lord is with you."*[124] Then Luke adds these words, saying: *But she was much perplexed by his words and pondered what sort of greeting this might be.*[125]

What does it mean to be favored of God? That's a good question. I mean, you would think that if you are favored of God that your life would be a bed of roses. But, evidently according to Mary's story, it doesn't work that way at all.

Listen as Luke continues: *The angel said to her, "Do not be afraid, Mary, for you have found favor with God. And now, you will conceive in your womb and bear a son, and you will name Him Jesus. He will be great, and will be called the Son of the Most High, and the Lord God will give to Him the throne of His ancestor David. He will reign over the house of Jacob forever, and of His kingdom there will be no end." Mary said to the angel, "How can this be, since I am a virgin?"*[126] This is interesting. Mary is not married. She's still a virgin. And she's going to have a baby. Is this something she should be overjoyed about? Think about it. Zechariah and Elizabeth had been married for many years. For most of those years they had been praying for a child. The birth of their son John in their old age was literally an answer to prayer for them. But, I doubt that the same thing can be said for Mary. She was just a single teenager and now, she was about to become a mother before she's married.

Mary and Joseph lived in a very strict community. Mary, actually, could have been stoned for being pregnant and unmarried. And imagine Joseph's hurt in the beginning before the angel appears to him to explain the situation. And, they are supposed to be happy about this?

Years ago a psychologist named Thomas Holmes developed a scale for measuring stress. He assigned numerical values to events that cause stress such as the loss of a job, moving to a new city or a new relationship. And another writer (Bridget Kuhns) took Dr. Holmes' scale and applied it to Mary. Here's how it adds up: A pregnancy - 40 points, an unplanned pregnancy - adds 20 more, a change in living conditions - 25 points, getting married - 50 points, a change in financial status - 38 points, and surely through all of it there must have been an argument or two between Mary and Joseph- at least 35 points, the actual birth - 39 points, change in sleeping habits - 16 points, change in eating habits - 15 points, not to mention all those uninvited guests: shepherds and angels coming and going and wise men from the East. Get the picture?

Now, Holmes says that people get sick when they reach 200 points on his stress scale. And Kuhns calculates that Mary's ordeal earned her well over 400 points.[127] This of course, does not even include the flight to Egypt, or the experience of watching her beloved son die as a common criminal on a cross. Is this what it means to be favored of God? Well, evidently being favored of God does not protect us from life's bumps and bruises. And that's an important truth for all of us Christians to understand. Mary was favored of God. But look at all the difficult things she had to go through.

So, if we are going through a difficult time in our life and we feel as though we can barely hold on, then we need to remember that God is very close to us just like He was with Mary. The angel Gabriel was not saying that God would make Mary's life easy. No, instead, what he was saying was that Mary would be used of God in an awesome way. That's what being favored of God means.

How about you? Can you say that right now you are being used by God for a purpose? Be careful about who you think is being favored of God and who is not. A person who is favored, or is being used by God may be going through lots of trials and difficulties.

Gabriel told Mary that she was favored of God and that she would bear a son. And Mary asked a sensible question: *"How will this be, since I am a virgin?"* And here's how the angel answered: *The Holy Spirit will come upon you, and the power of the Most High will overshadow you. So the holy One to be born will be called the Son of God. Even Elizabeth your relative is going to have a child in her old age, and she who was said to be barren is in her sixth month. For nothing is impossible with God.*[128] Underline that last sentence: Nothing is impossible with God.

Think about this, Mary in her embarrassment could have kept the visit from the angel to herself, but there was no way that Elizabeth who was far beyond child bearing age could make up a story about her pregnancy. It was a miracle, pure and simple. And Jesus' birth was a miracle, too. Nothing is impossible with God.

But we still wonder, why did God choose a young girl of childbearing age to carry His Son? Wouldn't that give us a chance to question this holy conception? Well yes, but that's so we will each have a chance to decide for ourselves. Was the birth of Jesus a miracle or not? Does God have the power to do such a thing, or not?

But, even if you are struggling with the idea of miracles today, well, I don't think God will hold that against you. What I'm trying to say is this: When it comes to God, be careful what you say is impossible. First, be careful when you start thinking about who is favored of God. Second, be careful what you say is impossible. And finally, be thankful that this young woman did say yes to God. Mary was free to say no, just as we are. God never forces obedience upon anyone.

You know, obedience isn't fashionable in our modern world, is it? Yet, it is an important part of the Christian life. And, in fact, there are some things that people would never do on their own, except that they believed that that particular thing was what God wanted them to do. For example, Chuck Colson was in North Carolina on Christmas Eve, 1985. He was there to speak in several prisons. He turned on CNN to catch the late news. On the screen was Mother Teresa. She had her arms around two emaciated young men. They were in the last stages of AIDS and had been released from prison to enter a home established by Mother Teresa's order. When a reporter demanded to know "why we should care about criminals with AIDS," Mother Teresa explained that these young men had been created in God's image and deserved to know of God's love.

Colson saw all this take place, and he wondered, "How could she do it? How could she embrace those men who were dying of that deadly virus?" And Colson knew he could never have that kind of courage. But, the next morning he had been asked to preach to several hundred women in the prison. And as he was getting ready to leave, the warden asked if he would visit Bessie Shipp, an AIDS patient in an isolation cell. "It's Christmas," explained the warden, "and nobody has visited her." At first, Colson thought, "I can't do this", but then, in his mind's eye, he remembered the face of Mother Teresa and he heard her words when she had said: *These boys deserve to know of God's love.* And so, Colson heard himself saying to the warden, "Well, all right, take me to Bessie Shipp." When they arrived at the isolation cell Colson discovered a petite young woman bundled up in a bathrobe, reading a Bible. They chatted for a few moments, and since there wasn't much time, he got to the point. "Bessie," he asked, "do you know Jesus?" "No," she said. "I try to. I read this book. I want to know Him, but I haven't been able to find Him." And, so, Colson took one of Bessie's hands while the chaplain took the other, and together they led Bessie in prayer. When they finished, she looked at them with tears flowing down her cheeks. "It was a life changing moment," says Colson, "for Bessie and for me." Three weeks later Bessie Shipp, a new creation in Christ Jesus, went on to be with her Lord. And Colson says he shudders when he thinks how close he had come to saying no to that visit that day.[129] Colson's life had been blessed immeasurably because of his obedience to God and that's the message of Mary's encounter with the angel Gabriel.

Mary, did you know? Mary couldn't have known where this encounter would lead her. But today, two thousand years later, we know that truly she was favored of God.

First, be careful when you start thinking about who is favored of God. Second, be careful what you call impossible. And finally, be thankful that this Jewish teenage girl was obedient to God. And, for us today, we need to know that following in her footsteps, is the key, to having a life that is truly favored of God. Amen.

END NOTES

[1] *Freedom Through The Yoke* by Rev. Billy D. Strayhorn
[2] Matthew 11:25
[3] Acts 4:13
[4] Richard Exley, The making of a Man, Honor Books, 1993, p. 12
[5] Sermon Illustrations, 1999
[6] Charles Swindoll, Growing Strong in the Seasons of Life, Zondervan, 1983, pp. 150-151
[7] Brett Blair, July 2005
[8] Jack Kuhatschek
[9] Romans 10:17
[10] Brett Blair, July 2005
[11] Matthew 13:44
[12] Matthew 16:25-26a
[13] Romans 8:16-17
[14] Matthew 5:8
[15] Alexander Solzhenitsyn
[16] Johnny Dean
[17] King Duncan
[18] Michael Yaconelli
[19] Bill Bouknight
[20] Nashville: Upper Room Books, 1996, pp. 29-30
[21] Christianity Today, Sept 14, 1992, p. 36
[22] Matthew 1:7-8
[23] Dallas: Word Publishing, 1995, p. 80
[24] Matthew 5:43-45
[25] Matthew 5:45
[26] 'End of the Road' excerpted from Every Second Counts by Lance Armstrong, People, Sept. 22, 2003, pp. 180-181
[27] Bill McCartney, with Dave Diles, Ashes to Glory; Nashville: Thomas Nelson Publishers, 1995, pp. 290-291
[28] Donald B. Strobe
[29] Parsons Technology, Bible Illustrator
[30] Luke 12:16-21
[31] Zechariah 3:2; Amos 4:11
[32] W Wiersbe, Wycliffe Handbook of Preaching and Preachers, Moody Press, 1984, p. 251.
[33] Genesis 50:19-20
[34] Genesis 50:20-21
[35] Jeremiah 29:11
[36] O. Dean Martin, Good Marriages Don't Just Happen, Old Tappan, N.J.: Fleming H. Revell, 1984
[37] Romans 12:1

[38] Romans 12:2
[39] Halford Luccock
[40] David G. Rogne
[41] Dr. Ernest A. Fitzgerald, God Writes Straight With Crooked Lines, New York: Atheneum, 1981
[42] Johnny Dean
[43] Johnny Dean
[44] Philippians 2:4-8
[45] King Duncan, adapted from Don Emmitte
[46] Donald Deffner, Seasonal Illustrations, Resource, 1992, p. 162
[47] Brett Blair, adapted from a sermon by Rev. C. Wayne Hilliker: 'Living A Life That Matters'
[48] John 10:10
[49] Chris Francescani, ABCNews.com, Oct. 5, 2006, Cited by Pastor Gregory P. Fryer
[50] Revelation 3:15-16
[51] Nathan Nettleton
[52] Frank Rothfuss
[53] Bob Tasler, Restoration: Confronting the Brother
[54] William J. Carl, III
[55] Matthew 18:19
[56] George E. Thompson
[57] 'The Sun to Shine and The Rain to Fall' by Rev. Richard J. Fairchild
[58] Matthew 20:6-7
[59] George E. Thompson
[60] Sermon Illustrations
[61] Philip Yancey
[62] Brett Blair
[63] Traditional
[64] Brett Blair
[65] Luke 13:1-3
[66] Luke 13:4-5
[67] Job 19:25-27
[68] John 11:25-26
[69] John 10: 27-29
[70] John 14:2-3
[71] Sunday School Times
[72] Exodus 15:11, 13
[73] Acts 9:34-35
[74] Acts 9:40-42
[75] 1 Timothy 1:15-16
[76] Acts 9:41-42
[77] Posted by Carlos Wilton on PresbyNet, 'Preaching Stewardship,' #1688, 9/16/99

[78] Matthew 6:33
[79] King Duncan
[80] King Duncan
[81] Today's Christian Woman,'What's Up, Doc?' 'Small Talk,' May/June 1996, p. 25
[82] Resource, July/August, 1990
[83] Mark 1:15
[84] Matthew 8:16-17
[85] Matthew 10:1; Luke 9:1; Luke 10:1
[86] Genesis 1:26-31
[87] Matthew 10:17
[88] Matthew 12:16
[89] Galatians 4:13-14
[90] Matthew 8:13a
[91] Mark 1:15
[92] John 5:7-1
[93] Matthew 7:24-27
[94] Matthew 24:43-47
[95] Charles Swindoll
[96] Matthew 5:3-10
[97] 1 Thessalonians 4:10-12
[98] John 20:21
[99] John 21:17
[100] Matthew 25:21;23
[101] Rev. Stephen Schuette, Salem Evangelical UCC
[102] Michael J. Silverstein and Neil Fiske with John Butman, Trading Up, London: Penguin Books Ltd., 2003, p. 38
[103] As told by the Rev. Jean A. F. Holmes, Nauraushaun Pres.
[104] Luke 6:38
[105] Mark 2:1-12
[106] Mable Newcomber
[107] Monte Unger, NAVLOG, January, 1975
[108] Romans 15:5
[109] Psalm 90:12
[110] Ted Koppel, Off Camera; New York: Alfred A. Knopf, 2000, p. 173
[111] Rev. Enrico C. Sartorio, Social and Religious Life of Italians in America; Boston: Christopher, 1918, pp. 52-53. Cited by Frances M. Malpezzi & William M. Clements, Italian-American Folklore; Little Rock: August House, Inc., 1992, p. 47
[112] Reader's Digest November 2003, p. 83
[113] 2 Corinthians 9:6-15
[114] 'Generous Hearts' by Linda McCullough Moore, Family Circle, April 1, 2005, p. 144

[115] By Amanda in My God Story, compiled by Bob Coy; Fort Lauderdale: Calvary Chapel Church, Inc., 2001, pp. 130-132

[116] Uncle John, *Uncle John's Bathroom Reader Christmas Collection;* San Diego, CA: Portable Press, 2005, p.125

[117] Isaiah 40:1-5

[118] Adapted from 'Matthew and the Matchbox Car,' by the Rev. Barbara K. Lundblad, 1996

[119] *Flash Points Igniting the Hidden Passions of Your Soul;* Wheaton, IL: Tyndale House Publishers, Inc., 2002, pp. 73-75

[120] Ronald W. Nikkel in *Fresh Illustrations for Preaching & Teaching,* Baker, from the editors of *Leadership*

[121] Dr. Shotwell

[122] John 1:4-5

[123] Composed by Mark Lowry and Buddy Greene © 1991 Word Music/Rufus Music/ascap

[124] Luke 1:26-28

[125] Luke 1:29

[126] Luke 1:30-34

[127] David Beckett, D.Min., 12/23/2001

[128] Luke 1:35-37

[129] Charles Colson, *Being The Body,* Nashville, TN: W Publishing Group, 2003, pp. 336-338